The Lady on the Chocolate Box

Gelaine Rohan

Published in Australia by Sid Harta Books & Print Pty Ltd,
ABN: 34632585293
23 Stirling Crescent, Glen Waverley, Victoria 3150 Australia
Telephone: +61 3 9560 9920, Facsimile: +61 3 9545 1742
E-mail: author@sidharta.com.au

First published in Australia 2023
This edition published 2023
Copyright © Gelaine Rohan 2023

Cover design, typesetting: WorkingType (www.workingtype.com.au)

The right of Gelaine Rohan to be identified as the Author of the Work
has been asserted in accordance with the Copyright, Designs and Patents Act 1988.

All rights reserved. No part of this publication may be reproduced,
stored in a retrieval system, or transmitted, in any form or by any means without the prior
written permission of the publisher, nor be otherwise circulated in any form of binding or
cover other than that in which it is published and without a similar condition being imposed
on the subsequent purchaser.

ISBN: 978-1-922958-19-8

*What lies behind us,
and what lies before us are tiny matters,
compared to what lies within us.*

— Ralph Waldo Emerson (1803–1882)

About the Author

This is my first book, written to ignite a lost memory. I grew up in 'God's Country' and still live in the shire.

On many occasions, I heard my mother telling her friends (while pointing to me): *I never wanted this child! I tried everything to get rid of her — I jumped up and down stairs, hoping to trip. I took castor oil with Epsom salts, and I prayed to lose her! Yet here she is!* Yes Mum, here I am, and this is my story.

I have a bucket list!
1. to ride a bike without falling off
2. to meet Kylie Minogue, and
3. to finish writing these pages.

Well, another — I would like to win Lotto ...

Writing these pages meant that I was stretching my damaged brain to its limits, trying to retrieve memories that had been locked away in a vault, unopened for years. While trying to fill in the missing pieces, some things returned easily, staying long enough for me to write about; others came only as a flash, often returning in the middle of night, waking me from deep sleep with an avalanche of memories. Controlling my emotions was sometimes hard when bad memories returned bringing panic attacks, nightmares and much anxiety — hadn't my life become hard enough? Many times while writing these pages, I wondered what I had started. It hurt so much and putting my life on paper was way too hard and confronting, but it also proved to be cathartic.

I am happy these days to be able to walk a straight line when on a pedestrian crossing. I used to zig-zag when over-correcting myself, unable to stay within the lines …

During this writing process I became aware that there were many things in my life that I had never been able to talk about, yet now I was writing about them. In a way, the very thing that nearly killed me became the thing that saved me. I have learnt how time does not always heal but can help some of us to endure.

Dedication/Acknowledgements

This book is dedicated to my daughters.

A special thanks to Dr Chandler, the neurosurgeon who literally gave me back my life — without him, I would not have been able to do any of this.

Thank you to my cousin Angela, who helped me find the correct words; also thank you to Zanthea. Both typed endless pages from my scribbling when I was unable to use a keyboard.

Last, but not least, my thanks go to the lady on the chocolate box, who is always in my heart.

Author's Note

Meaningful memories and people have found their way onto these pages, and I've tried to word them carefully so as not to write them in a negative way. Some people still remain in my heart, yet they no longer have access to it. When people have asked — 'Am I in it? Can I read it?' — it's then that I feel a little exposed.

After my brain haemorrhage and strokes, then surgery, living inside my own head space meant I was frequently in overdrive and going off course. I became aware that I had to control my emotions after realising I'd developed a vulnerability or predisposition to any phobia lurking in the sidelines, purely because confronting the fear and emotional turmoil was all part of my recovery.

After nine years spent detailing my life in all its shades, I feel that I have become a better person. In the process of writing, I became aware of how I had previously lost myself in a fractured lifestyle, and in that same process, I 'found' myself, so I now refer to this as the time when I met me.

Preface

My mother gave birth to my sister during the Second World War on Boxing Day 1944 while my father was in Borneo with the RAAF. Surrender came on 15th August 1945 when our greatest enemy — the Japanese — had been held back in battle for three days, and the second world war was declared over. My father arrived home to God's Country on December 13th that same year to meet his first-born child, my sister, who was now eleven months old. The next day, while proudly taking her Christmas shopping, he was photographed and their picture was front page of the *Sydney Morning Herald* the next day; my sister, cover girl at just eleven months! I was born five years later. My sister and I, referred to as Baby Boomers, had parents who were wholesome people as individuals, but together they were toxic.

There were many 'productions' in our house, and my sister and I both attended school with bruising and welt marks from our parents' many emotional outbursts; my father's coming from war neurosis and my mother's, I can only assume from a dysfunctional and loveless childhood. For many years my sister and I were unaware that we were a little different from most other families. My mother unknowingly was named the 'Sutherland Screamer' by my father. She thought herself a loving mother, often telling everyone how much love she gave to my sister and I, but in actual fact, I didn't know what a mother's love was. As a little girl, I became aware of her panic attacks, and I learnt what a palpitation was. As a teenager I became aware that my needs were not a priority when I was being stalked by a boy I knew, who said that he wanted to kill me so that nobody else could have me. This fell on deaf ears, and I was told not to bring any further embarrassment on the family.

It was not until a young mother myself that I learned what a mother's love truly is. I witnessed how Mum was able to shower my daughters with affection — the kind of love that I had craved but had never received when I was a little girl.

As a mature woman, I became preoccupied with *her* needs, *her* wants and *her* expectations of me, which caused my life to ascend and descend into a rollercoaster-like pattern that revolved around hers. Anticipating Mum's needs was a distraction from my own unhappiness until a life-changing event robbed four months of my life.

After leaving hospital, many months later at home with my memory returning, my sister suggested I write things down to help retain them. Months turned into years, and with no balance and no strength to keep myself upright, there were plenty of falls, both physical and emotional. Not being able to use a computer keyboard, I kept handwriting memories because it was the only thing that I was able to do on my own.

This became a self-fulfilling prophecy; however, luckily for me I had no idea of the mammoth task I had undertaken. Now, some ten years later, my writings are quite a novel. My first clear memory that returned was of my first day at school, so this became the beginning of my journey.

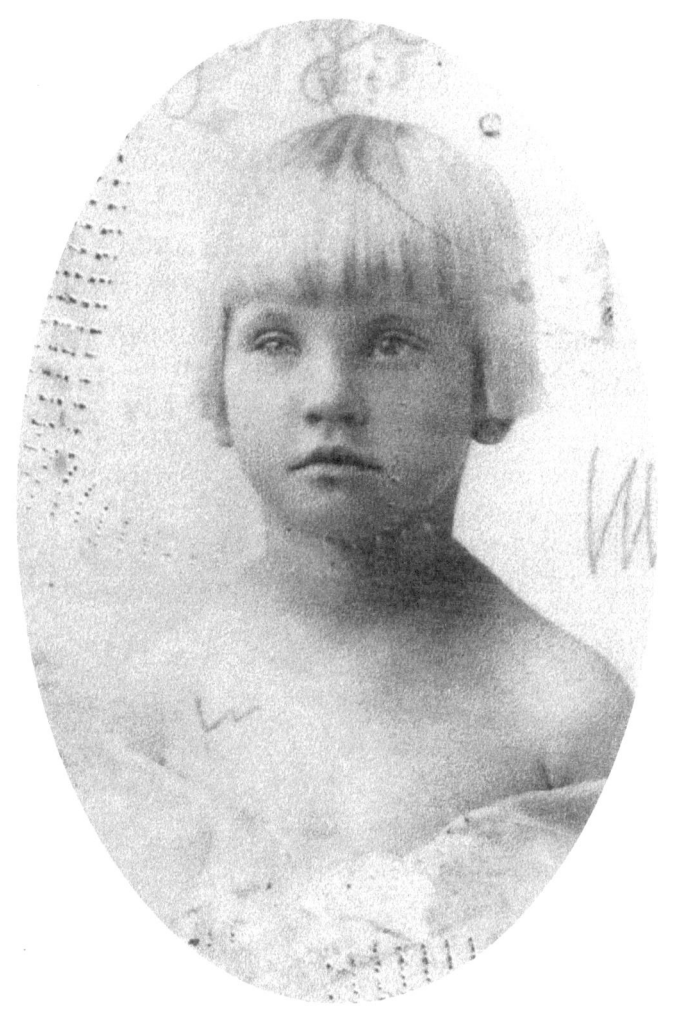

*The Lady on the Chocolate Box.
My mother, 1923.*

My father comes home from New Guinea

My parents soon after my father returned from World War Two — happy days! (for a while)

Our home in "God's Country", 1955. Now replaced with two storey medium density dwellings!

Chapter 1

Christmas Day is only a week away. This year there is so much more excitement than simply the approaching Christmas Day. Today our harbour is in party mode with family and friends all gathering in the city to welcome home their hero husbands, sons, brothers and even some women — mainly nurses — all returning home from the Second World War.

My father is one of these men returning home after being away in New Guinea serving eighteen months in the Royal Australian Air Force (RAAF). On this day, our famous Sydney Harbour Bridge in the heart of Sydney is decorated in streamers and balloons, dressed to party. People are overjoyed, dancing in the streets with music coming out of the windows of the tall buildings. People are frolicking in happiness.

More excited than most, and with good reason, was my mother, there to greet and welcome home her husband of only three years with their firstborn child, who was born while my father was in Borneo. This little baby is now eleven months old and today will meet her daddy for the very first time, so it is so much more exciting for my parents than for most. This baby is my older sister, and I can barely imagine the atmosphere on this day after such a heartbreaking time in our history. That day, my mother would be reunited with her husband, separated by war a week after finding out that they were to become parents. Now a year later, they were more excited than the night they first met, which both had told me about on many occasions.

Over the years I had been told about this night and how, while war was happening, my mother and her friends would go into the city to dance in the Trocadero in Sydney's George Street. Each girl would wear their favourite dress, and when the sailors and boys in uniform came into town, it was an exciting time. It was one of these nights when my parents met; my father was home on leave at the time and went to the Trocadero looking for the most beautiful girl in the room and his eyes fell on my mother in her purple dress (her favourite colour).

My father told me that for him, it was love at first sight. Obviously, it was the same for my mother because just six weeks later, they married at St Jude's Anglican Church in Sydney's eastern suburbs, close to where my mother had been raised by an auntie.

My mother had found love with this handsome air force man, Jack (she eventually preferred to call him Johnny). When married, my mother moved out of her auntie's house, and my parents rented a little room built onto the side of someone's house in the inner west. Sadly, just a week after learning they were going to have a baby, my father was sent to war for a possible two-year period. During her pregnancy, my mother was very ill and unable to even hold down a glass of water, so her mother moved in to look after her.

This may have been a good thing, because my mother had not spent much time with her mother, who was unable to even change a nappy, so as a baby, Mum had been given to an auntie to be raised. Her mother then returned to her party lifestyle in the city bars — drinking whiskey, playing the piano, dancing with men and smoking cigarettes held in a long gold holder as well-to-do French ladies would have done. Maybe this flair was inherited from her French mother? I have heard that she was a real party girl, strong-minded yet popular, with a jolly personality, loving to always have *fun fun fun*.

My mother's father left when Mum was given to an auntie to be raised. Who really knows why she gave my mother away — was it to party or was it out of love and to have my mother raised in a family lifestyle?

Now, on this day when my mother is waiting for her husband at Circular Quay with their newborn baby girl to meet her daddy, it is such a special day for them.

The following day, my father took his baby daughter into the city, and while doing some Christmas shopping, was noticed by newspaper photographers who were scouting around the still-excited city. His photograph was taken and was on the front cover of the next day's *Sydney Morning Herald*. My sister, a cover girl at just eleven months of age! My parents were so happy living in bliss, both unaware of the neurosis that my father had brought home, nor the anxiety that my mother carried within from her neglected childhood. Many years later these issues would almost destroy their marriage and each other.

It would appear that for now, things were running smoothly and four years later my mother discovered that she was pregnant again, this time with me, so it was time to look for a bigger place to live. Both my parents had grown up on the beach, my father being a lifesaver at Newcastle beach before joining the air force, and my mother growing up close to the eastern suburbs beaches.

The land closest to any beach available for them to purchase was at Sutherland in the heart of the shire, better known then as 'God's Country'. They purchased a large block of land for just 200 pounds and my mother designed our new home, which we moved into when I was almost four. My sister was enrolled in the new little school just around the corner and up the hill; I would join her some years later.

I have often wondered that if I grew up in another suburb closer to the beach and I went to a different school, and had different friends, would my life have been much different? Would I have had different outcomes? Would I have had the dramas that came into my teenage years? Maybe it would have been worse.

Is our life planned as they say? Did those years teach me

resilience? As a child I was not strong of mind; however, it may have taught me the resilience and mindset that I would need for the fight of my life when I was fifty-three.

Chapter 2

My first memory of school is of being in a classroom standing shoulder-to-shoulder with other kids, all in line along a wall under a window. I remember feeling a little afraid of the kids, whom I had never seen before this day. My sister had been going to school for a few years already; I wondered which room was hers and I remember wishing she were there with me because I was afraid of the people I didn't know.

A girl that stood in the line beside me had black curly hair; I had only ever seen that kind of hair on the golliwog dolls that our father bought for my sister and me — our father liked golliwogs, calling them 'fuzzy wuzzy angels' and telling us they were good people. (I have since learned what fuzzy wuzzy angels are.) I didn't know then what a golliwog was, but, on this my first day at school, I wondered about the girl beside me with black curly hair, thinking, is she a golliwog? Kris and I became good friends over the years, and now, in our mid-sixties we still talk to each other on the phone. When we were little girls growing up, Kris often came to my house to help with jobs that I had to do before my father arrived home.

Jenny was another girl I met on this day, who often wore a dress that was much too long. Over the years at school, I called her 'always-in-trouble Jenny'. When we were little, I thought she was very brave because she wasn't afraid to let the teachers know how she felt about them ... and school! Jenny and I became good friends, and we also still talk regularly on the phone. I last saw Jenny a few years ago at her husband's funeral.

Over the following year, my parents became president and secretary of the Parents and Citizens school group. A woman who lived around the corner was treasurer, perhaps due to her husband being the very much respected local bank manager. They had a son in the same class as me, so when a P&C meeting required our parents to be at the school, I was baby-sat by this respected man. Our parents had become good friends, especially our fathers, who bonded over their mutual love of orchids, and they would often exchange different species.

In the fifties there was much concern in God's Country because there reportedly was a man frequenting a lane at the western side of Sutherland near the Woronora River, where young couples would go for secret cuddles and kisses, and most likely, other things! They were being stalked and attacked. There were many warnings in the local papers telling young couples to stay away from this place where this terrible man had been sneaking up on people to watch, then he'd attack them with a weapon. The perpetrator would drag the boy out and tie him to a tree, where he would then rape the girlfriend in view of him. This had happened a few times, so now God's Country was spoiled with such goings on, and the shire was in the news for all the wrong reasons. Everyone was talking of the 'River Rapist' who had to be caught. Concerned parents began warning their teenage children to stay away from the bush areas.

Due to there being very few female police officers in the fifties, and in an effort to catch the rapist, this meant that two policemen were to pose as a couple pretending to be smooching in the car, with one of them dressed in female clothes, at least from the waist up! During this plot, the River Rapist pounced on the car, not knowing that there were two burly policemen sitting inside. A scuffle broke out and the rapist surprised police by having a gun. Shots were exchanged, police believing they may have shot him while he was trying to escape. Feeling sure that he was wounded and that he may soon seek medical attention, the police waited for him at the new local hospital.

Back in the bush, however, the River Rapist soon made it to the road, managing to be picked up by an elderly couple, who noticed when they reached the main road that he had passed out, presumably from loss of blood. Not aware of the man in the back seat's identity, they did see that he urgently needed medical attention and the couple drove him to the hospital. Soon he was in court, tried and sent to prison. This became big news, and effectively tainted God's Country.

In the aftermath, parents were devastated, especially mine

because as it happened, this so-called River Rapist was the same man who had been minding me when Mum and Dad attended school meeting nights. The incident became the talk of the shire; the rapist's wife was comforted by many, but to add insult to injury, it was later discovered he had also been stealing from the bank when a large sum of money was found buried in the soil of his orchids. I wonder what my father must have thought, but I imagine he then realised why some orchids had been for exchange and others were not ...

At the rear of our yard was an uncovered drain where my sister and I played. We caught tadpoles in the murky water, occasionally pulling leeches off our skin. One day, we got more than we had bargained for when we found a brown duck with a flat, cream-coloured beak. Our mother was out and our father not yet home from work, so we took it into our bathroom to wash in the bathtub with Sunlight Soap. To our surprise it became a white duck! When our mother returned home, she said we could keep it, so we called it Donald (of course), but when it began laying eggs, our mother suggested we put an 'a' at the end of her name. She was now our egg-laying Donalda and became my companion. On some days, she followed me to school. In the 1950s our school very often had fete days to raise money. On one such an occasion at the fete, I won first place for the child with the most unusual pet. I had walked Donalda to the fete on a lead, dressed in a bonnet, tied with a pink bow around her neck and bows around her ankles. She was quite a feminine little duck and I think she enjoyed being dressed up, showing off on the walk to school, pleased to now be getting a break from the old pram that I sometimes pushed her around in.

At home, she became the boss in our yard after fearlessly winning her fight for leadership against our cattle dog Smokey and our mother's cats. Nor was she afraid of the German Shepherd dog around the corner; she would fly into him to scare him away when he sometimes tried following me to school. She also loved my father's classical music and one of the very few times I saw my parents laughing together was when Donalda would run up and down our driveway quacking and fluffing her feathers, almost as if dancing to the music of Beethoven, which was played loudly. Our mother said Donalda was disturbed because the music was too loud, but my father said she was dancing along to the beat. Sometimes, when my father was not able to play his music (because my mother had smashed a supply of his records) Donalda would waddle up seven steps to our backdoor and repeatedly quack ... asking for the music? My father certainly loved his music.

After my first year at school, my sister began high school, which was a long way from home and walking there meant that she had to cross over the railway lines on her way. This now meant I had to make some new friends and walk all by myself. I was afraid without her around because meeting others was hard for me. I was painfully shy, so I lacked social confidence. My mother often told me about the trips to the

Chapter 2

shops when people stopped to talk to her and I would hide behind her, and cry, sometimes hiding under her skirt. My sister was much more friendly than I was; she was the social one, who spoke to anyone and everyone. My mother said my sister would 'talk to Billy the Blackfella, but not this one' — she always said that pointing to me. I don't think that a great deal has changed over the years.

I have remained friends with a few girls from my early school days and another of them is 'always in trouble Jenny' — the little girl who wore the too-long dress. Jenny lived in tiny little shack with her mother, two aunties and an uncle on the other side of the bush. The shack was up the hill from the big ponds and the waterfall that came off the creeks from the Royal National Park. After running into pipes carrying drain water underneath the highway, the water would spill out on the other side, splitting into two sister creeks. One creek ran by the front of our house through the little park in the middle of our street, the other ran through our backyard, then it continued on for a few more blocks to finally meet up again and flow over a huge rock forming a waterfall into a massive pond where, on most days, we swam with leeches, tadpoles and tortoises.

Another friend who lived across the road on the other side from school was Brenda, who had two brothers and a younger sister. We also have remained friends and still speak by emails or phone chats. I liked her parents and my observation at the time showed that she came from a happy, stable family ...

unlike mine. My parents were now screaming daily at each other and my mother going through the house slamming every door was a daily event.

I was also friends with Lynette who lived down from our house on the corner of the busy street. Her mum became a friend to my mother. Lynette's brother became a policeman and when we were little, we were all in awe of him.

Luckily for me, our school was not a school where pupils had to wear a uniform, so I was able to wear long sleeves or slacks to hide the many bruises and welt marks from my parents' temper outbursts. This meant that even in summer, I was dressing in long sleeves and slacks to cover marks on my body from the *4x2* — a plank of wood measuring four inches wide by two inches thick and around a metre in length. My sister and I often got a belting with the *4x2* from our father when a job had not been done to our mother's approval.

My friendship with Jenny probably developed from us both being unhappy little girls, Jenny had no father and sadly, a mother who caused great embarrassment for Jenny by coming to school with a weapon to abuse the teacher on the many occasions when Jenny got into trouble, which was quite often. Sadly, this made Jenny the laughingstock in our class. I always felt sorry for her, and I befriended her. We became best friends, and she also came to my house after school to help me with the chores from a list my mother had left for me.

I sometimes also had help from another friend in my street — Robbie — who lived just a few houses away. Robbie had a stutter and a dribble and some of the nasty kids in our class called him 'spazo'. I now realise he had cerebral palsy. I was often laughed at and called 'spazo's friend' for caring and defending him when he became upset from the other kids' taunts. His mother owned the little flower shop at the side of the funeral parlour near the big shops. She walked past our house each day on her way to work. I remember her over-bleached hair and bright red lipstick. Her name was Rose, and I thought this was because she grew so many of them. Her backyard was a maze of many beautiful flowers to which I would help myself when my mother needed comfort.

When my sister began high school and I was a little older, our mother got a job managing a lady's fashion shop in Sutherland. Soon, she was coming home tired and always in need of something...

Along with Jenny, Robbie would help me complete my jobs so I wouldn't get into trouble, and we were warned by Robbie's mother: 'Do *not* go into the flower beds and touch the flowers.' We still did! We would raid them daily, then walk up the hill and cross the railway lines (before the days when all railway lines were fenced off) and take flowers to the cemetery, putting flowers on the kids' graves that no one had placed flowers on. When we ran out of Robbie's mum's flowers, I remember we then searched for wild freesias and pogonias.

My sister left school and began working, so, getting dinner ready became my job. Besides that, she was having regular epileptic seizures, which caused some difficulties.

My mother was often sending me 'to buggery', as she called it, when I tried to snuggle up to her at night and I *hated* the way I felt when I saw her embrace other kids. She was known for her love of children, but I never felt love from her when I was a little girl. She was very emotional and demonstrative when smashing things and screaming, however, in some areas she was quite guarded.

There was another boy in our street, living two houses down — Paul — who had two younger sisters. The youngest sister had died from a disease that we were told had been caught from the drain, and yet we were still allowed to swim and wade through it, catching tadpoles. The creek that meandered down our street eventually ran into the bush where we spent all day running through it, swimming and floating on tyres taken from Paul's dad's garage.

My parents, most of the time, seemed to have no idea where I was or what I was doing. That's how it was then. In the fifties, children were always told: 'Get out in the beautiful sunshine. It's good for you! Children should be out in the sunshine and not in the house.' In those days, there was no such thing as block-out to prevent sunburn; no Slip Slop Slap, as it is now called, and as long as the sun was out, I was not allowed to stay in the house. That suited me, because staying out of the house meant I was free from any screaming that was often happening within our home.

My mother and Paul's mother, Lilly, became good friends,

and when my sister and I were getting the *4x2* from Dad, our mother would run to Lilly seeking comfort. It was a sad day when later, Lilly died in hospital from complications after surgery. I sometimes feel that my mother never fully recovered from losing her friend. Paul's dad remarried around two years later; a woman who had three daughters of her own. One of them was Zannah, who became best friends with my sister. She was closer to my age, but much more mature than me. I was a tomboy and very immature, but Zannah was grown up, having more in common with my sister. However, the three of us were good mates and she would come to our place, and we'd play our girly songs on my father's home-made hi-fi system. We'd sing along to the girly love songs; the three of us singing into our hairbrushes like the Aussie version of The Supremes. My sister and I could not hold a note if our lives depended on it, but Zannah was a good singer, and we taped her singing *Sad Movies* by Susie Thompson using our reel-to-reel tape deck.

On weekends, as soon as my jobs in the house were completed, I was sent outside. spending the rest of the day with Robbie and sometimes Paul, swimming and splashing around in the creeks running down to the bush. We caught tadpoles to take home to watch grow into frogs, sometimes getting lucky and catching a tortoise. Every day was spent pulling leeches off each other and when it was time for toileting, it was much easier for Robbie and Paul being boys. In my need for privacy, I had to squat behind the fattest tree. We were mates, staying in the bush until almost dark because I wasn't allowed back in the house. Robbie and Paul never watched when I went behind a tree, I guess it was part of our mateship.

These days, God's Country has many units and medium-density dwellings, but when I was a girl, everyone lived in houses that had their own backyard and every second house had a mulberry tree. Days too cold for swimming, or on rainy days, Robbie and I climbed and raided these huge trees. Before Paul's mother died, he would come with us, and on these days, after gutsing ourselves, we'd return home loaded up with bags of mulberries, which were given to Paul's mother to make mulberry pies. We also gathered a collection of silkworms in cocoons, which, according to my mother, grew into moths so they had to be kept in my cubby that I had decorated under our house. I imagine they would have enjoyed life a lot better in the quiet of my cubby house anyway, just as I had felt at times. When my mother was doing a 'production' as I used to call them, I often hid in my cubby in search of peace and calm in my little part of the world. My escape there would bring comfort with a feeling of safety, and a sense of belonging.

One night, after a mulberry tree raid, I woke more than once through the night experiencing severe rumbling in my stomach followed by cramping and projectile red vomit, filling my bed and painting the walls and carpet. My mother came into my room in the middle of night to attend to me, now covered in purple yuk. She would scream: 'Oh my God! Christ Almighty! These haven't even been chewed up! Just swallowed!' She then would pull the sheets off my bed, now also full of red berries and I was made to run cold water in the bath to soak the sheets for washing the next day. In later times, I had to wipe down the walls and scrub patches of carpet also still carrying the tell-tale purple stain that remained for years to come. That was so very long ago, and I have never eaten mulberries since …

When Mondays came with the return to school, I would take my silkworms to sell for a penny. I sold the ones in a cocoon for twopence (two pennies); sometimes I could sell a big silkworm for threepence each! This gave me money to buy a bag of lollies or an ice block like the other kids did on the way home from school. My mother found out though, so I began telling lies, saying I got ice blocks from other kids. Eventually I got caught out and I had to write two hundred lines — *I must not lie* — and my father said that I should give the money from my silkworms to my mother to bank for me.

In the late fifties when television came to some homes, Paul's family was one of the first in our street to have one, so after my jobs were completed and Jenny and Robbie had gone home, I would go to his house to watch *The Mickey Mouse Club* show until my father got home from work around 5.30 pm to let me in, so that preparation for dinner could begin.

Everyone had an outside toilet, and our outside toilet

had a horrible man's face in a frame on the back of the door. My sister told me he was a brigadier. I didn't like his eyes — they seemed to follow me wherever I went. The outside toilet was referred to by our dads, for obvious reasons, as the thunderbox. Flushing toilets were only in hospitals or the big shops and some posh houses. The 'Dunny man' — also more respectfully called the 'Sanny man' — came twice a week to cart away our toilet's contents. Dressed in overalls and with a large leather-like bib covering both shoulders, he would carry the now-full toilet bin on his shoulder out to a truck waiting in the street with full cans of other home's waste, replacing it with a clean shiny bin in preparation for next week's poo.

Since our toilet was outside, going to the toilet was not reason enough to gain access to the house, nor could I use thirst as an excuse when our outside laundry was also locked, since my mother had a plumber come to our house to install a bubbler behind our laundry. This was her attempt to keep us outside after my sister and I had gutsed ourselves on packets of jelly crystals, not to mention the hidden creme biscuits that we found. Being locked out meant that the vegetable preparation for weeknight dinners had to wait until my father arrived home from work to let me in.

At school, after I settled into class, I enjoyed my time there far more than my time at home. These were my happiest times. I began winning running races, high jumps and long jumps. Winning most events easily had helped me grow self-worth and I became very popular, soon representing the school in most field and track events at sports carnivals. Also, winning at swimming in the pools at Cronulla beach. I have since seen the same sporting success in my youngest daughter. My popularity in school was far better than at home where I would often be writing: *I must not give cheek to my mother*, which would be written out and under my father's strict supervision at least one hundred, sometimes five hundred times when I had answered my mother back. I was often in trouble for not cleaning something properly or for forgetting to bring the washing in from the line. My latest writing punishment was *I must not guts myself with mulberries*!

On Saturday mornings, my sister and I began learning physical culture, a lesson with yoga-like exercise done to music and popular in the sixties. Lessons were held in the little hall attached to the church in the next block from home and was the closest my sister and I got to any church on account of my father's dislike of God, after being at war, which had upset him deeply.

Because of the way Dad felt about God, my sister and I were not allowed to attend scripture classes at school, and we were made to sit in the library. My father told teachers that we were *not* to worship a god who allowed wars to happen. My father never showed any physical damage, but as I grew older, I became aware that he had been quite profoundly emotionally wounded. As a little boy, he was raised a Roman Catholic, but returned home from war a tortured man, a heathen. My mother, doing what was felt to be the right thing, had my sister christened while he was still away at war, but five years later my father did not allow my mother to have me christened in church, so I never was. We were *never* to enter a house of God whom he now felt hatred for. He told me of the experiences of Hellfire Pass, and though he was not in the Pass, he knew some men who had been; he hated the Japanese and often told me never to trust any Asian man. Lucky for us, we were now allowed to go into church grounds to learn physical culture because our mother had encouraged him to let us be like the other girls in the shire. My sister won the big zone competition called Champion Girl. All girls from other clubs in the shire competed against each other until, through a process of elimination, the best girls were selected to compete for the title. Both my parents were overjoyed and so proud when my sister gained first place. Because I saw them so happy, I promised myself that I would also win, hoping to make them proud of me too.

After a few more years of learning 'phissy', the day of my competition arrived, and I was covered in bruising and welt marks. Nothing unusual for me, it was the life my sister and I were living — all normal to us. On this day, my mother covered my marks with tanning lotion and lucky for me I went through each elimination heat and also on to win. So now I also was Champion Girl. My parents once again were so proud, this time of me. My mother proudly telling everyone: 'This is my other daughter who has won, just like her big sister.' She was even more proud the following month when I won the club championship for highest point scorer over the year. The many trophies, medals and certificates I proceeded to win over the following years are now kept safely in a suitcase under my bed — the very case my father had taken to war. These days it is filled with my special things and little treasures, including the gifts of love made for me by my children over the years.

During my childhood I often heard my mother say: 'Johnny has war neurosis' — I thought this was a medal of bravery and wondered why she had never shown it to me. I often thought about the horrible stories of war that I wished my father had never told me. The ones about the Japanese troops bombing Darwin caused me to panic when a plane flew overhead. I thought it was going to drop a bomb. He also repeatedly told me: 'Asian men are cruel men and *not* to be trusted!' Of course, he was only referring to the Japanese and the Hellfire Pass. I thought anyone who had different eyes to me was Asian; I was young and didn't know anyone with Japanese eyes, so I had nothing to be concerned about.

Most of us growing up in the fifties and sixties had a father affected by war, but we were far too young to understand how they had been affected by what they had been through and too young to appreciate the horror of war. So, except for the drama that was about to come into my life, the sixties would have been a good time to grow through.

Our mother was making new friends and a name for

herself in the fashion shop that she now managed. She was a stunning-looking woman then, becoming known as the pretty lady with the lilac eyes. I remember how I loved watching her apply her makeup, and after she applied red lipstick, she'd begin smacking her lips together. Also, because of her beauty, some people referred to Mum as the 'lady on the chocolate box'. She was not only pretty, but positive and driven, and despite her angry outbursts (productions) she had an outgoing and jovial personality with confidence plus. Who would know where this came from? Maybe this was a cover up from her apparently miserable and loveless childhood, having not been raised by or shown love from her own mother. My mother's love language morphed into the teaching and expectations of my sister and I to clean the house. During her childhood it seems she was made to feel loved and needed by doing housework. I think she thought that my sister and I would also feel loved and needed by being provided the same upbringing.

A goodnight kiss was only given from my mother when all jobs were done to her satisfaction, which was perfection, and trying to tell her any news of the day was not allowed because she was 'far too tired to listen', so when I became frustrated and spoke loudly to her, I was told: 'Cheeky girls grow ugly, just as you are becoming so you can go to *buggery*.' I soon thought twice before speaking up for myself — not wanting to be an ugly girl or sent 'to buggery' yet again. Many times, I was taken into the bathroom and told to look in the mirror with my mother telling me: 'See how ugly you are becoming?' while she held my head so I had to look straight ahead into the mirror at myself. I'd then repeat the mantra: 'Yes, I am getting ugly, so I won't give cheek anymore.'

I was a bed wetter until I went to high school, going to bed each night unhappy and terrified of the sandman, who I was told was coming to take me away in his big black sack. I knew he was real because I heard him knocking at our door, and my mother sending him away soon after I had gone to bed when he came to check up.

When I was in Grade 5, a man came to our house selling pills and lotions. He became good friends with Mum and Dad and was soon invited to stay over on Saturday nights. On occasions he had touched me inappropriately. I became scared of him and very uncomfortable around him. When I told my mother, I got into trouble for saying terrible things about a nice man. My next punishment was five hundred lines of — *I must not say bad things about a nice man.*

Many years later when I became close enough to my sister to tell her about him, she told me he had also touched her and she also was not believed, so now all these years later I can see that my mother was unable to face a situation where she needed to protect us, opting instead for the easier pretence of some things not happening, then she had no need to deal with it.

My sister and I were very often told that little girls are to be seen and not heard, and most nights we were writing all sorts of lines like — *I must clean the house properly. I must not give cheek to my mother! I must not guts myself on mulberries! I must not say bad words about Uncle Jack* (this is what we were told to call him). *I must finish the housework before I go to school ...*

Even though I enjoyed the school environment more than home, I was late for school every day and unaware the teachers were documenting it. One day, when I was told to take my jacket off and roll up my slacks for a race, the sports teacher noticed welt marks and bruising on my arms and legs and told me to turn around. He then called the headmaster rather loudly, saying, 'Come and take a look at this!' That night, the sports teacher came to our house with the headmaster, and I was sent to my room (but listened with the door ajar). I heard the police mentioned and thought that maybe they were coming to get me, so I got into bed to hide under the sheets where I pretended to be asleep and eventually, I did.

I couldn't wait to grow and finish school, get a job and save money to move out, like my sister was doing. I was looking forward to high school because my sister had enjoyed her time there and was working in a butcher's shop in the city. She told me she was saving to leave home because she'd had her share of hurt. For many years I was unaware of her unhappiness; we were not sisters who spoke much to each other with five years and nothing in common between us.

Sadly, when my sister was diagnosed with epilepsy, our mother became focused on a possible cure and began building my sister's confidence by telling her how beautiful she was, often telling me in front of my sister: 'You should be more like your beautiful sister.' My mother was boosting my sister, unaware it made me feel inferior. I wanted to be my sister, complete with epileptic seizures. My mother's encouragement to my sister was not so good for me to witness, but even though I had very little self-esteem, I had confidence in myself. Years later, when I became a mother myself, I was able to imagine my mother's pain and curious nature and considered myself lucky that my children and I had escaped such a sick thing.

I remember many nights spent at the new hospital because my sister, on some days, had more than one convulsive episode from an epileptic seizure. This must have been very hard on my mother. I think it was around that time when I saw my mother's temper truly coming to life as she would go through the house slamming every door. My father often said, 'There goes your mother again, in full flight!' and he would follow with a screwdriver, taking every door off. This meant that for many years we had no internal doors inside our house because they were all stacked in the garage. Years later, my mother reminded me how the first door to be replaced was the bedroom door, so maybe it was the making up which my father enjoyed. My father was a deeply obsessive and overemotional man, expressing all kinds of emotions and having no shame in exposing any of them. He was also a very clever man and made small cabinets and bedside tables for around the house. He was also proud to tell everyone of his love for my mother, his movie star wife! My mother was often putting on a 'production' or having a palpitation attack with a hot sweat.

When in bed on one occasion because of great concern over something that had made her 'sick', I picked some flowers for her from our Jacaranda tree. This was her favourite tree because of its lush purple flowers — she loved anything purple. When I put the flowers in a vase on her dressing table, the flowers dropped off and the sticky sap from the flowers ate into the varnish on the top of the dressing table. I was in great trouble for being so stupid. Seems I couldn't do anything right. I am now sure that my mother was suffering anxiety attacks, but nobody seemed to know much about these attacks back then. Given her loveless childhood with a mother unable to raise her, I wasn't ever curious about her mixed bag of emotions, my hands already full.

I was in Grade 6 when my mother's mother, Lydia — my nan — came to live with us. Prior to Nanna's arrival, her sister — Auntie Annie — had also been living with us for six months and though they were sisters, the two old ladies were also fierce enemies. They often would hit each other, pull hair and call each other names like *bitch, slut, whore,* and *gutter tramp*! Oh yes, my sister and I very quickly learnt swear names. My father would often have to separate them from rolling around on the floor, pulling out handfuls of each other's hair and punching into each other as boys would fight in the school playground. When my sister and I were sent to our room, we watched from our slightly open, sliding bedroom door, and I, in particular, thought it was very funny to watch these two old ladies having a punch up! I'm not ashamed to say I can remember laughing so much when watching them that my sister told me harshly, '*Shh*--be quiet'.

I think there may have been a jealous streak in Annie, because Lydia was the youngest of thirteen children and very spoilt. My mother had told me that Nanna always got what she wanted with her determined nature and headstrong attitude. During the First World War, there was much anti-German sentiment and Lydia's parents had been distraught as three of their sons were at war and stationed in London, which sadly, was bombed by the Germans.

After the war, when Lydia was eighteen, she fell in love with a soldier and wanted to bring her new love home to meet her parents. They were delighted and looking forward to meeting this man who had captivated their headstrong and difficult child. Being in love had further exposed her determined ways and she wanted to marry this soldier. Her parents both knew that to try to stop her may have brought on a fierce battle because she was now old enough to marry without their consent. They also knew that Lydia would go ahead and marry him regardless, so they thought it was best to meet him and give their blessings. They were suffering enough with their sons fighting the Germans who were now 'The Enemy' since bombing London, and so they were keen to meet this nice young man whom she wanted to marry.

When the day came, they set the table for a pleasant morning tea. I'm told that my great grandparents dressed up in good clothing to meet him; my great grandfather, a proud Englishman, wore a tie and a hat as gentlemen did in those times. They were looking forward to a lovely morning; my great grandmother having made fresh-baked biscuits and teacake to impress this soldier and welcome him into the family. But they were very soon shocked and devastated — he was a GERMAN soldier — the enemy!

Her parents could do nothing, and against all objections, Lydia and Lenny were soon married. Then, to add insult to injury, they lived in her parent's house, which for her father, being the proud Englishman, was an embarrassment to say the least. Not only were they disappointed in 'Liddy' but now they had the enemy living in their house. I have since heard about Lydia's parents being very rude to him, throwing his dinner plate on the table at dinner time and suggesting that he choke on it.

The following year when my mother was born, Lydia was unable to even change a nappy, and at five months, my mother was handed over to one of Liddy's sisters who had no children of her own. Lydia was quick to return to dancing in the city bars; the party-girl lifestyle that she had been living before and after meeting her soldier husband. Before long, her soldier husband left, moved interstate and changed his name, their marriage over. My mother never saw her father until she was sixteen years old, only to meet him by a complete fluke.

Years later, living in our little house in God's Country, my mother had taken her mother in to care for her and I have often thought how huge a role it must have been for my mother; one with great expectations. From a party girl who couldn't raise her own child, my grandmother Lydia now lived with us; how lucky for her that my mother didn't hold a grudge.

Nanna was still living at our house when I reached sixth grade. One day at school, I was sent to the art room for punishment after talking in class. My teacher came in, closed the door behind him and pushed himself against me, putting his fingers in my mouth. I could feel the front part of him against me while his fingers were pushing in and out of my mouth. My sister had recently told me all about sex when my mother said I had no need to know, so I knew what he was thinking about and I thought how rude he was and I became afraid of him, so, I bit down very hard on his fingers. I could taste blood! I pushed past him to get out, through the classroom to run home, while feeling afraid and crying. When I arrived home, I found my mother in a panic, crying with a neighbour comforting her while now waiting for an ambulance to take Lydia to hospital because she had collapsed when leaning over the bathtub to do some hand washing. I never saw my grandmother Lydia alive again, as an hour later at the hospital, she died of a cerebral haemorrhage. So, I never got my chance to tell Mum about what had happened.

That night, my sister and I were taken to the hospital to say goodbye to her. My day had been terrible, and I didn't understand why we had to say goodbye. I thought my mother was mad because we were told that Nanna was dead and dead people couldn't hear! I have never lost the memory of how I felt and how Nanna looked, appearing to be asleep; the calmest I had ever seen her, with a sheet up to her neck and a red rose on top of her chest.

The year after that, Auntie Annie took ill and was placed into an aged-care facility in the next suburb, so my new after-school outing for distribution of flowers with Robbie was a visit with a bouquet for her.

The next year would be my first year in high school and I was very excited and couldn't wait to get away from the teacher I had bitten. I was soon experiencing the worse feelings I had ever felt when Mum told me I wasn't going to high school because I wasn't clever enough, and now she was saying, 'You may see how important it is to do homework!' How was I meant to fit it in with all the housework that had to be done? I didn't have time for homework. I remember I cried for a long time when learning I was not going to high school with the friends I had made. After that, I spent a lot of time in my cubby house because I didn't want to be in the same space as my mother.

The following year, again in primary school and repeating

my Grade 6 year, I stayed best friends with Robbie, whose mother had the lovely gardens. She was always very nice to me when I went to Robbie's, and she'd have flowers that I often gave to Mum. Now I didn't want to give her any more flowers because she had denied my dream of going to high school and I was not only disappointed but embarrassed as well. Robbie didn't go to high school, instead, he went to work with his brother for three half days per week. We remained friends and when I arrived home from school, we would take flowers to the aged-care facility where my great auntie was now living.

Saturdays became our cemetery visit, but since there was someone now home on a Saturday, we picked freesias and other wildflowers to put on the graves. These days, I think of Robbie in late September, the time of year when freesias are blooming, and the smell jolts my memory back to days spent running around the cemetery with him, looking for decent flowers to pick.

My sister was having seizures on a regular basis, which was doing a lot of damage; she was often in hospital when she threw more than one seizure in the same day.

One day I was woken by my mother's screaming, to find my sister locked with a twisted body on my mother's lap while having a convulsive episode. This day, she had almost bitten my mother's finger down to the bone. My mother had put her finger in my sister's mouth to prevent her from biting down on her own tongue, but my sister had locked jaw on my mother's finger and the floor was covered in blood. My mother was screaming out in pain. I won't forget feeling great panic for my mother and sister, so I ran into a neighbour's house for help. After this event, there were pegs in each room of our house to be put in my sister's mouth, in the hope to prevent such a thing happening again.

Events such as these, have stayed in my memory.

My parents were always screaming at each other, and mostly, when the 'productions' began, my friends would run home to get away from the yelling and from my mother who would go through the house slamming all the doors and throwing anything in her path that was not bolted down. If my father was home while this was happening, he would go into the garden and chop all her flowers off, sometimes pulling them out roots and all and he'd throw them around the yard. This would inspire my mother to smash his Beethoven or Mozart records, and so the productions went on … and on … and on. Sometimes, if I was able to, I would sit under the house in my little cubby. I remember being very shaky, and scared. There were productions every night in our house.

My father called me Bagshot. I don't know where this name came from, or if it had any particular meaning. When I asked him, he told me it was just someone special who he had read about, and he called me this until the day he died. Not very flattering and yet I think it may have been a term of endearment. My girlfriends were called Sweetheart, Love, Princess or Blossom and I was Bagshot! For a little girl like me who was told how ugly I was becoming, to me it was just further confirmation of my ugliness because it sounded like an ugly name. Sometimes, my mother called me Murtle Maglaganpus, telling me that Murtle was a sulker, and since I was a sulker like Murtle, it was a good name for me because I was 'forever sulking over something'. I was having many unhappy days at home, and yet, amidst all those times, there were good times.

One of these good times was the way our street celebrated the Queen's birthday in June, back then called Cracker night, or Bonfire night. Our street had the biggest bonfire, built in the park at the top of our street. Large planks of wood were first built in a tepee style by Danny, who lived down on the next block across the street from Robbie's house. We all added to it, building it to be the biggest around. Danny dragged tree parts up to it and over the following weeks it was added to by the dads in the street, so when Cracker night arrived, we had the biggest stack of material waiting to be lit. Someone would always put a car tyre on top to make a lot of black smoke on the night. We all had our own bag of fireworks and people came from all the adjoining streets to share fireworks and join in the fun of our fire. We were all told not to put any flames near the big electricity pole that was close. One of the dads hammered a big piece of wood into the ground for the fireworks needing to be nailed onto it, like the ones that spun around. If there was no rain, the fire would be glowing for days and we would take bread to toast on long-handled forks.

In our excitement to toast our bread, we saw no danger in the still-glowing embers from nights before and our parents didn't show any concern. But thinking back, it may have been because Paul's dad was a fireman, so I imagine that all trust was placed in him.

When television came into our street in the fifties, it changed all our lives, and the Saturday afternoons when Paul, Robbie and I would go to the local School of Arts hall to 'the flicks' as they were known then, was now over because my parents said there was no need anymore. Robbie and Paul were relieved because the last time at 'the flicks' I had screamed like a lunatic while watching the shower scene in *Psycho* and was told by someone to, 'Shut up or piss off!' I finished up under the seat trembling in terror to escape the screaming from Janet Leigh, who was being brutally stabbed while in the shower. This was long before classifications. The vision of this scene stayed with me for many years, giving me a fear of knives. Lucky for me I had no idea of the terrible ordeal involving knives that was about to come into my life.

Chapter 3

The following year, I finally got to high school and just as well I was unaware of the huge turning point about to come into my life. School itself was nothing like I thought it would be. Apart from meeting my lifelong friend, Ruby, there wasn't much about this school to keep me happy. However, life at home was a little better since we had also recently become a proud household with a television. My father loved the man shows.

Most of our mothers watched and loved a morning home show called *The Del Cartwright Show*, which was about budget shopping and home decorating. My mother was invited to appear on this show as a guest to show her cleverness in making home décor items of plastic flowers draped over the awkward shapes of driftwood that my father would collect from the beach when he went fishing. We were so proud to tell everyone that our mother was on television. Now she truly was my father's movie-star wife! Television became our new entertainment, and this meant that my sister and I were relieved of the night-time talkback on the radio, also the serials about Greenbottle and his two mates who could not get along with their neurotic teacher. So, relief came when the radio was exchanged for 'real' entertainment. But our television became a bargaining item and was used as a coaxing apparatus to manipulate the order of events in our house regarding housework and punishments.

In those times, the television stations would close at midnight and a man's voice said, 'Thank you for watching'. Then, the national anthem would play (*God Save the Queen* was our anthem in those times), after which, the Queen would appear on horseback before the picture would cease with a little dot appearing on the screen. There were many days that my sister and I were punished by not being allowed to watch a favourite show, but I worked out that if we snuck into the hallway, and if the sliding door into the lounge room was open, we could watch shows that were reflected onto the mirror in the hallway opposite the lounge room. We did this for many nights before we were caught, so we saw a lot more than our parents were aware of.

On many occasions, my mother had to go to hospital with sweats and palpitations, or to take my sister after an epileptic seizure in which she had hurt herself in the fall, and it was in those days that I decided nursing was for me. Hospital seemed like a nice place where the nurses were all respected and appreciated, so I decided I wanted to become a nurse and work in a hospital. Even when my mother told me I couldn't be a nurse (because I didn't do my homework), it didn't deter me. I knew that I would be punished if I missed my jobs at home, and with my sister now a working girl, and unable to do housework, all jobs became my responsibility. Besides, my poor sister was often having a seizure and doing a lot of damage to herself, breaking her teeth and her nose time and time again.

When I first began high school, I didn't really like it much because a lot of girls came from other schools, and I had never seen them before. Being such a shy girl made it hard for me to make new friends, so apart from meeting Ruby, I didn't make any new friends in class. I began to enjoy my walks home each day though, which took about thirty-five minutes if I went the correct way and didn't cross over the railway lines. After a while, I became aware of a boy who was always at the corner milk bar when I walked past in the afternoons. He would always say hello and began to ask me if he could walk me home. He didn't take no for an answer and walked with me regardless, asking me about people I had not met. The next morning, he would be at the bottom of my street to walk with me to school. Then, in the afternoons, when school was out, he was waiting near the school gate to walk me home. This happened every day and I asked him one day, 'How come you don't go to school like the other boys do?' He said that he had to work but was going to leave his job because he didn't like it. I told my mother about this boy who walked with me even though I had said no when he asked, and she said I should just ignore him. But I was not able to do that when he showed up every day and walked with me regardless.

After a few months at school, I met Tina, who lived a long way from the school, so she had to travel by bus each day. One Saturday when my mother was out, I went to Tina's house to help her cook biscuits with her mother. I thought this is how a 'normal' family acts, and in those times, I thought that every family was normal except for mine (and Jenny's). I was happy to cook with Tina and her mother for the large family they had. Her mother was nice, and I liked her straight away. She was a short lady, a little overweight and very pretty with very dark curly hair. Tina told me that her mother was Fijian and Polynesian; I liked her because she talked a lot more to me than my own mother did. I know Mum did love my sister and me, but we were told on many occasions that little girls should be seen and not heard. Neither of us felt love from our parents.

I enjoyed talking with Tina's mother and she began telling me about her son Ross, who was never home and stayed out late. She then told me that he had fallen out of a train a year before. This had damaged his head, cracking his skull. She told me, 'The accident seemed to destroy such a loving and thoughtful boy who is now entirely different. He gets so cranky and irritable and has developed really bad attitude.' A few hours later, her son turned up. To my shock it was the boy who had been following me. He was all smiles when he saw me and asked why I had not told him that I knew Tina. Well, I didn't back then.

Chapter 3

That afternoon, he caught the bus with me to the shops where I would walk home from. I saw a boy I knew, and I began talking to him, and when I did, Ross began pushing him around, telling him to stay away from me, or else. So, I then began to feel a little scared of Ross and was able to see what his mother must have meant. After that, I was glad I didn't see him in a long time — I thought he was staying away from me because I had cried and yelled at him to stop pushing my friend around. After a few weeks, I asked Tina about him; she told me he had gone to stay with an older brother for three months. I heard that he was in a detention place for under 18 year olds for theft. I was relieved with him away because he had frightened me when he pushed my friend around and I wondered what gave him the right to do that.

At high school, I was slowly making new friends and we would all meet on Sundays to catch the train to the beach. Having spent so much of my childhood years in the surf with my father, this is what I loved doing and it was all the more fun now that Ruby was always there. I enjoyed her company, and we instantly became best friends, so she was able to tell me that her mother had died just before she began high school. Poor Ruby, then I knew why she was so quiet back when I first met her. I had thought she was shy like me, but she was sad without her mother. Soon it was 1964 and in November I would turn fifteen, I was enjoying life and my new friendship with Ruby.

My favourite day was Sunday, especially in the summer

months, because this was our beach day. We caught the train and met up with new friends from other high schools who got in at various stations along the way, so I was beginning to meet other shire girls. The trains were called 'red rattlers' with no lights inside and sliding doors that stayed open unless you closed them. Usually on the way home from the beach, a few of the boys would hang out of the doors, showing off while the train sped along. Little wonder that Ross had fallen out one day. The girls would usually be grabbed by one of the boys in the dark tunnel and this was referred to as 'the grope'. My goodness, why would they have wanted to grab any of us? We all looked like aliens with our red sunburned faces and no eyebrows, because in the sixties it was fashionable to pluck them all out. Looking like aliens didn't stop the boys from trying their luck with the grope though. I remember being fearful that this may happen to me.

We all enjoyed music, and all had transistor radios, so music was a big part of our lives. Elvis Presley was the most popular recording artist, but most dads disliked Elvis with his pelvic thrust, which was considered disgusting, and most thought he couldn't sing even though he sometimes sang nice gospel songs. Some mothers, and most of us girls were crazy for him, and the older boys wished they were him. My dad would say, 'Mark my words, he won't last, he is just a flash in the pan,' adding that we didn't know good music. It was a shock to our dads when Elvis was invited to appear on the biggest entertainment show on television — *The Ed Sullivan*

Show. The show was sent by satellite about a week later for viewers in Australia. Ed Sullivan had all the big stars like Sammy Davis Jr., Frank Sinatra, and now Elvis. When on television, Elvis was only to be filmed from waist up because of his 'pelvic thrusting' — such wicked movements that I think the dads were perhaps a little jealous of ... Now, almost forty years after his death, he is still the king of Rock and Roll music. Quite an achievement if you ask me, and hardly a flash in the pan.

On the walkway from the station to the beach, there was a fun parlour in the arcade with a jukebox, pinball machines and dodgem cars. The boys all loved the dodgem cars, driving them around to loud music, bashing into each other. Some were close to the age that would allow them to drive real cars on the roads; they couldn't crash into others then.

Another form of entertainment were clown heads that would turn from side to side with the open gaping mouths to throw balls into. Best of all though was the juke box, and all of us girls would wait in line to put money in to select our favourite song, which would play out loud. I think everyone down on the beach could hear the loud music playing ... We all carried transistor radios with us, so we had loud music not only in the train, but also when we were on the beach. Music was a big part of our lives, and we were all influenced by the songs. Most of us girls were designing our bodies around the tanned bikini girls that the Beach Boys were singing about, and we covered ourselves in baby oil or coconut oil, sometimes both mixed together, to lay out in the sun, hour after hour — in order to burn! No Slip–Slop–Slap in the sixties, in fact, a tan was considered healthy. The boys tried surfing, some were better than others and were called 'surfies'. Some of the boys in the older crowd had their own cars like the ones in the songs being sung about. The boys who thought they were tough called themselves 'Rockers', and often there was a battle between the Surfies and the Rockers.

On the way home from the beach on the train, all of us girls would lift the legs on our shorts, to see which one of us was the lucky one with the most sunburn. We all had red burnt faces (with no eyebrows) and we all were smoking ... well, that was the 'mature' thing to do. We must've looked like smoking aliens ... I enjoyed growing up in these days — good weekends.

Mondays at school was post-mortem day, where there was a run-down of relationship dramas and where boyfriend troubles were dissected. There was serious talk in the playground between girls telling others how they had to end it with their latest boyfriend. Any excuse would do — he blew his nose too much or spat or maybe he groped another girl in the train on the way through the tunnel. I was lucky because I didn't have a boyfriend and didn't want one to worry about how to end it. If a girl wanted to end going steady, she could usually find any excuse. One girl I knew ended it with her boyfriend because he didn't like The Rolling Stones. These were good days with my friends and days looked forward to, and for me, freedom from that silly boy Ross.

Ruby and I became 'besties' in our second year of high school. The same year that my sister got married and we also both became friends with two of the boys in our group — John and Frank. They were best mates who lived just around the corner from each other. On our days at the beach, Blind Freddy could see how John and Ruby were falling for each other. Frank was nice looking, very quiet, and a bit shy of girls so there was only small talk happening between us. Frank knew Ross … well, everyone knew or had heard of Ross. I was developing a crush on Frank, and only told Ruby this because I had heard Ross was soon coming home and I was afraid of causing trouble after the last boy had been pushed around just because he spoke to me. So, I hadn't told anyone since having heard things about Ross that were not very nice. I was hoping to leave school before he returned so he wouldn't know where to find me. I knew school would be the first place he would look for me when he did, and I was dreading having my freedom and my fun days messed up by him.

Things had settled down a bit at home and my mother was much calmer since my sister had married in the previous year and was now expecting a baby. I'd given her quite a few fluffy toys that I had won at the fun parlour. We were all excited about this news, and my mother in particular was the happiest I had ever seen her while waiting to be a grandmother. She began buying baby clothes and anything else my sister needed.

My sister and her husband lived in a little garden flat in Cronulla and when my sister gave birth to a son in November, our mother was besotted! Sadly, my sister's marriage was short-lived. They had been having problems and when her son was five or six months old, her husband didn't come home from work one day and she never saw him again. My poor sister thought it was because she had had a few epileptic seizures that may have frightened him away. No one will ever know because there has never been any contact. Our father took my sister out west to his parent's home in the hope of locating him, but they were not forthcoming with any information. My sister moved back home with us, and my mother was now able to help raise this little boy; I noticed a softness in my mother that I had not seen in our home before now.

In my third year of high school, we had exams which were then called the Intermediate Exams. In fact, in the sixties most girls left school after the exams. Only the high achievers would stay on, mostly to achieve good marks in the following year to become a private secretary or stenographer at a busy city office. While some chose to leave to pursue a career in hairdressing, others (of which I was one) wanted to become a nurse and some did achieve this, but not me. Girls were not encouraged to get a great job, after all, back in those times — most girls were only going to marry and have babies, which is why most of us were taught good housekeeping and cooking skills, with most parents hoping their daughter would marry a boy with a good job.

Chapter 3

These days, women are going to university and gaining themselves a good career. Some are running a business and outdoing the men. Some, even running the country! I have a friend who is a business manager taking her to England, China, Japan and New Zealand for corporate meetings.

Big things were happening in the sixties and the biggest band in the world, The Beatles, were coming to Australia to do concerts. They were nicknamed the 'awesome foursome'. I was almost sixteen and my pin-up boy out of them was the drummer, Ringo Star. On the day they arrived, my sister and I were allowed to go to the airport to see them land and the crowds were huge! But it was raining heavily at times, and as if that wasn't enough, we didn't get to see much because my sister had an epileptic seizure in the crowd. We were taken to a hospital until our parents were able to pick us up a few hours later.

The following year, I left school and was lucky to get a job in the new, very large shopping complex just built in the shire. My mother was pleased I was in ladies' fashion, though she really would have preferred for me to get into hairdressing, even finding me a job in a hairdressing salon. No way would I do that, because if I couldn't be a nurse then I wasn't going to be what she wanted.

I was much happier to be working these days. My parents were unaware I was saving to move out. But best of all, there was no Ross who had now been sent away yet again — a great relief for me as I was thinking about his bully-boy behaviour. And at the end of that year, I had a birthday, turning sixteen.

Growing up in the sixties was a time of many changes, and not just in my life, because all our lives were affected by the goings-on. Apart from my sister having a baby, and the new shopping mall where I was able to get my first job, there was the changeover to decimal currency as well as the 'Man on the Moon'. Much was happening, too much to mention. Our prime minister, Harold Holt, vanished in the ocean while swimming near Portsea in Victoria on a hot December day in 1967. Women's Liberation was getting lots of attention, with women now starting to stand up for their beliefs, burning their bras and showing independent strength without men. Hippies were singing about flower power. What was flower power? I still don't know! Smoking LSD was talked about, and I didn't know what that was either, yet there were songs about it. The Vietnam War had caused much heartache with boys being conscripted and I was glad not to have a brother made to go to Vietnam because some of my school friends had been upset and crying over a brother who had been called up for war duty. The poor boys had very little training, most never having seen a gun or weapon, but now were having to use one. Young men were forced into going to a war they knew nothing about and told that it was 'not our war to be fighting in', and yet, boys were conscripted by ballot. This was done by recording their year of birth then month and day, and then through a selection process, they were notified by mail. Of course, most didn't want to go and who could blame them? Those who didn't comply with the rules were called 'draft resisters' or conscientious objectors, many of whom along with protesters were fined or jailed. We knew some older boys who were drafted and had to go to the war and fight. They may have had a father like mine, who came home from war traumatised from terrible experiences, then it must have been horrendous, not to mention terrifying for the boys and their mothers. So much was happening in the sixties.

The thing I remember, and which upset me very much, was the death of my friend Robbie who had started work with his brother and had an accident on site that killed him. I was not allowed to go to his funeral because my parents said it would upset me even more and I can recall the terrible loss I felt. I cried for days but was told to just stop crying and get over it.

I made a few new friends at my job, which was unusual for me, but I think it was because I really liked it there and my boss lady was very nice. One boy who worked in the fashion section was learning to become a window dresser and had appeared on the television show *Number 96*, so we all wanted to be his friend, except for me. He asked me out, but I said, 'No way.' I was understandably a little unsure of boys.

Not much later, sadly, I began to hate the job that I had loved. I found out that my boss had enrolled me into a course to learn how to become a department buyer … without even asking me. When I fronted her about this, she said it had been already discussed with my mother, who had given her permission, but what about asking me if it was what *I* wanted? I was never asked! Did I not exist?

After this happened, I began developing some defiance and soon had enough money to move out of home. When my mother wanted to bank the money I saved, I bought myself a horse so she couldn't get it as she had done in the past. Having a horse meant I could ride with Kris (fuzzy wuzzy) who was exercising a horse for her neighbour. Also, Jenny was minding a horse for a boy she knew who was leaving his horse in the paddock at the back of the garage she lived in. He told her to ride it whenever she wanted to because he was afraid of this crazy horse.

Well, Jenny wasn't afraid of anything, so we all had great fun riding together. It was just so normal in the sixties to see horses being ridden in God's Country and we often rode out to Cronulla Beach, where we would gallop over the huge sandhills at the northern end of the beach called Wanda Beach. These sandhills were enormous and seemed to stretch for ages, running from the beaches to the back of the oil refineries at Kurnell. We took almost an hour to reach them from home. We rode out past the shopping mall where I had my first job, and the new hospital where I would much rather have been at learning to be a nurse. Our horses must have been tired, but once there, we galloped along the beach and over the many huge sandhills that stretched for miles and miles. My mother told me that a movie called *Forty Thousand Horsemen* was filmed on these massive sand hills.

Chapter 3

One day, when we arrived at the hills, we were shocked to see dozens of police cars and ambulances there, and the hills had been sectioned off with police tape. The police stopped us galloping over our hills and ordered us to leave immediately. There had been a murder of two little girls. With all of the events in the sixties, now there were the Wanda Beach murders.

Chapter 4

Although I rarely saw him, I found out that Ross had been away again, for nine months again, but in an adult prison. Secretly, I had missed him. Why? Was it because he said nice things to me? My life experiences since have given me a possible answer — even though I had seen a bad side of him, he had sometimes made me feel special with the nice things he was always seeing in me. At home, no one said nice things to me, so I wasn't feeling loved by anyone. Tina told me that he would be back home soon. While he was away, I found out that he had been in a detention place yet again, this time for breaking into a house. I never told him about knowing this, not wanting to expose anyone for telling me. Still, I hoped he would stay away from me and not show up at my work as he had done before; Ross had been coming into the department where I worked, only to walk past me three or four times every day. Then, every afternoon, he was waiting at the railway station to travel home with me. I was embarrassed by him always showing up at work and soon I was wanting to get away and leave that job too. It seemed that

Chapter 4

everyone who came into my life also was controlled by Ross. Another reason for leaving work was that I didn't want to do the course that my boss had enrolled me in, mainly because it was held in the city, and I was concerned travelling that far on my own.

Even though most of my friends from school had now gone into different areas for work and some of us lost contact with each other, the Wanda Beach murders had brought us all a little closer and we were all looking out for each other. I remained friends with Jenny, Kris and Ruby who all worked in a place on the way into the city with a few other girls who had gone to our school. I didn't want to work there with them though, because it meant travelling sixteen stops instead of three, giving Ross the opportunity to also get onboard the train, checking that people weren't talking to me. I knew his level of control and how he operated, and I was afraid he would create a scene.

When my friend Brenda from primary school had work in the city, she became involved with a new group of friends. We still saw a lot of each other on most weekends, though not every weekend like before, since now she had a boyfriend from out of town. On the weekends, Kris, Jenny and I were going for many horse rides. Ruby and I became best friends, and we were spending a lot of time with John and Frank. Ross had been 'away' at least three times and when he returned this time, he began asking me to the movies. Time and time again he asked, driving me crazy. Although I often told him

I wouldn't be allowed to go, he persisted and when I relented it wasn't long before he was back to his old tricks, telling boys to stay away from me. Even though I was a little afraid of Ross, there was something about him that fascinated me, and I knew he would never hurt me.

One day, he came to my house with flowers and waited for my dad to arrive home so he could ask him if he could take me to the movies. My dad said, 'Yes she can go, if you bring her straight home,' to which Ross replied that he would. Ross came the following afternoon and had brought along a record for me, a song called *When A Man Loves A Woman* by Percy Sledge. All these years later, an eerie feeling washes over me when I hear that song played. In the sixties, our music was on a little round vinyl disc and was played by turning it around under a needle that ran through grooves on the record to echo out a sound. Very different now!

When I met him for the date, Ross seemed very quiet. I wondered how detention must have changed him. Dressed up in a long-sleeved shirt, I thought how nice he looked. He was good looking, and I had recently heard a story going around that another girl, a friend of his sister's, also liked him. When we went to the movies, he was well behaved and treated me like a princess and, he didn't even swear in front of me, which was sort of a big deal then. Pleased that he had asked my father to take me out, I remembered how his mother said he had been a kind and loving boy before falling from the train, so I thought this was the Ross that she had spoken about. This date with Ross was one of a few firsts. On this — my first date — I was to experience my first kiss.

While Ross had been away, I enjoyed the beach every Sunday. My parents were not aware of the fun I was having with school friends because I didn't talk much at home. My mother was obsessed with her little grandson, so no one in my family knew that Ross had been in detention as I hadn't told anyone about things going on in my life. Sometimes I would tell things to my sister, and it was usually for advice. So, aside from my sister, and Ruby, no one knew about my crush on Frank. I had only told Ruby because I didn't want Ross to find out, since I was aware of his jealousy of other boys, whom he pushed and punched when they came near me. My parents were also unaware of the Saturday afternoons I had been spending at John's place with Ruby, while he and Frank worked under the bonnet of Frank's FJ Holden. What a car it was! Dark grey in colour, brown door on the passenger side, and a bonnet painted green on one side. Quite unique in appearance, it could not be missed, and was Frank's delight. John, Ruby and I often went out in Frank's car, and I thought he was a good driver.

At home I had learned to only speak if someone was interested and these days, my mother was busy with her new grandson, which meant she was not interested in much else. Saturday afternoons now were far better than going to the movies with Robbie and Paul when I was younger, which had been a real thrill. On these Saturdays at John's place, his father would show Ruby and me the garden, telling us about each and every plant: their names, and how to grow them. John had really nice parents — normal people who didn't scream and yell or smash things belonging to the other. How nice it was to see them laughing together when they sat near the radio, having bets with each other on the horse races. Ruby and I did not escape the nature lessons because we were also given a lesson about the heritage of all the birds in the aviary. We would laugh about it later, saying, *How come he thinks we want to know about the plants and stuff?* We didn't really want to know, but it gave us more to laugh about ...

Frank and I were only friends; he was good looking, quiet, very shy of girls, and had good manners. He had a good job, and respect for other people, all things that I was aware Ross didn't have. I liked Frank, but he wasn't my boyfriend, and he hadn't asked me out, so I didn't know how he felt about me. So, I went to the movies again with Ross.

He had been a gentleman the first time he had taken me, but this time when he came to pick me up, I noticed something different about him — he had been drinking. And on the way to the movies, he showed me a large knife that he was now carrying with him. I became very scared because it had a long blade like the knife in the *Psycho* movie, and I had never forgotten how the movie had me under the seat screaming in fear! Ross assured me that he was carrying the knife only for protection, telling me about a man in prison who had told him to get one just in case he needed to use it. His mother was right to have been concerned, as when Ross turned eighteen it meant no more detention centre but prison with adult men — a real worry for her that he could meet older criminals who may corrupt him. Her concern was justified. I was shocked that he carried a knife, but he promised again that it was only for protection, and we went to the movies.

At the pictures that night we saw some boys we knew; I said hello to a few of them and Ross became very jealous, asking if I'd been out with any of them and been kissed while he was away. I had never been kissed by anyone, only by him on our first night out, a long time previously, and now I felt a little afraid to say anything at all in case he got upset with me. On the way home he kept asking me what was wrong because I was very quiet. I grew brave and told him that I didn't like that he had tried touching my private parts during the movie and I had felt uncomfortable about him carrying a knife, and it frightened me. I didn't want to see this side of him, so I told him that he didn't need to carry a knife.

'No one else does!' I finished angrily.

I was seeing another side to Ross, but still felt that we had something in common and I liked the things he said to me that made me feel special. He always told me what he liked about me, and it was a nice change from my mother, who told me I was getting ugly from speaking up, and how I should dress up to be more like my sister, not dress like a boy, wearing jeans, but I should wear a skirt and some make-up. She would conclude with the last instruction to: 'Get rid of that *bloody* horse and start acting like a girl!'

She was happier now as a grandmother, bringing much relief for us all because until then, she had been a bit crazy at times and my father had told me on many occasions that he loved my mother, but he would go fishing on most nights to escape her screaming. Although he loved her deeply, it was clear he was needing time away from her screaming. He had his own emotional problems and told me he was relieved that Mum seemed more settled with the arrival of my sister's little boy. She was so happy to mind him at nights so my sister could return to work, and I saw my mother give so much love to this grandchild.

One time at the movies, Ross tried to get me away from the boys I knew by taking me over to buy me an ice cream. During the movie he was agitated and tried again to touch me in places I wouldn't allow. He asked me all through the movie if I had been out with any of the boys while he was away. I thought the reason he was now very agitated was from having some beer before he picked me up, recalling that he seemed a little drunk and a bit funny (peculiar) when he arrived at my house, so I decided not to tell him that my parents had gone away for the weekend.

After the movie, we walked home in the dark, Ross repeatedly asking had I been out with any of the boys while he had been away. Then he asked if I had had sex with any of them while he had been away, telling me again about the men in prison who taught him about knives. *Sex? Are you joking?* I thought. I told him that I'd only been kissed by one boy and that was him. I also explained my fear of knives and why, which prompted Ross to laugh loudly. 'Oh God,' he said as he laughed. He thought it was funny! Funny?

When we reached my home, Ross insisted on coming into the house, and I couldn't stop him, so he soon was aware that my parents were not there. A struggle began when he tried to get more than a goodnight kiss, saying he had no intention to hurt me.

I was scared, but I stupidly ran to my room, sliding the glass door shut to get away from him, but he followed me and when I wouldn't open the bedroom door, he smashed it and got in. He came at me, pushing me onto the bed, trying to kiss me. I was terrified because he was in a rage and had been drinking. He looked crazy mad, and he had a knife. He seemed to be confused that I was afraid of him, telling me that it would be okay. *What would be okay?*

I knew what he was after because my sister told me all about sex. I was so afraid that he would use the knife on me, so I screamed, hoping the neighbours would hear and maybe phone the police, but the screaming from our house was all too normal.

I fought to get him off me, pushing and punching him, telling myself that I wasn't afraid of him, but I *was*. He hit me hard ... I saw stars and think I was knocked unconscious because I recall him holding me, with no memory of getting into his arms. My nose was aching, bleeding, and my head was throbbing, there was blood, and my entire body was in pain. Ross was crying and holding me tightly very close to him. I was too afraid to push him away. He was sobbing and begging me to *not* hate him, telling me that he loved me and was sorry. Saying over and over, that he loved me and didn't *want* to hurt me. He left while he was crying. I heard the front door slam shut.

None of the neighbours were aware of what happened that night in the house. Any other time, the police were called, but no, not this night ... I was sore and throbbing all over and noticed blood on the bed cover, then realised where this blood had come from. I felt as though my body had been run over by a truck, glad that he was gone. I knew I needed to wash the bed cover and clean the glass from the broken door off the floor; my parents would return the following morning.

While crying and shaking, I struggled to clean the bedroom up. The glass from the broken door was now all over the floor and hurting my knees, then I began to throw up. *I wished my sister would come home!* I was unable to phone for the police because only our neighbour had a telephone, and it was too late in the night to go knocking on their door. Feeling I couldn't walk into their homes in such a mess, I also didn't want to tell them about anything that just happened anyway. I was unable to do anything about it that night.

I went to the police early the next day to tell them because I thought they were my friends. But when I told them what had happened, I was disappointed because they told me I would not be able to charge him as I had no witness. And an assault charge had to have a witness, they further informed. What about my black eye and swollen nose? The police told me I could have him charged with aggravated assault if I'd had a witness.

The next day, when my parents arrived home, I told them I had been bashed up by a girl from school who thought I liked her boyfriend. My parents wanted to know her name, so I made one up and told them that I had smashed the glass door when I got home because I was angry! I was, in fact, worried about what might happen if Ross found out that I had told the police. The only people who knew about that night, except for the police, were my sister, Ross and myself. I often wished I had told Ruby.

The police assured me they would see that Ross stayed away and I begged them not to tell my parents, saying that I had lied to them about my black eye and the broken door, and my mother would punish me if she knew the truth.

Chapter 5

My black eye faded as the weeks passed by. Whenever I was with Ruby, John and Frank, I felt safe. None of them knew of the flashbacks I was having of the night after the movies and the event with Ross — I had told nobody the full story, saying that I smashed the door in a temper. I told Mum and Dad much the same thing, knowing that they'd believe me, because apparently, I was a 'chucker' or a 'smasher' just like my mother. After the event, Ross came to my work again one day; I told him to stay away from me, but of course he didn't. So, with a good measure of defiance, I left around two weeks later.

My mother was pretty upset with me for this, which I didn't care about. I was lucky to get a job closer to home selling lottery tickets and newspapers in a little gift shop close to where my mother was working, who, by now, had told my new boss what a disappointment I was for leaving what had promised to be a good career in sales. I felt ashamed, even though I hadn't done anything wrong ...

I felt relief at the new job because the police station was

just on the next block, which I thought might work to keep Ross away. Working on Saturday mornings meant I was now unable to attend my Saturday morning Physical Culture classes. This meant joining a different club to have lessons after work on Monday afternoons. The new place was at a hall close to where Jenny lived on the edge of the bush, but as luck would have it, soon, Ross found out and began turning up to walk me home every week.

He still begged for forgiveness, and I realised that there was no getting away from him. None of the other boys would talk to me because he had warned them off (except for Frank). I think he was afraid of Frank because he was so tall and much quieter than most of the other boys. It wasn't until much later when Ross had turned up at the beach wearing a singlet, that I noticed he had my name tattooed on his arms and I knew then why he had arrived at my home in the past wearing a long-sleeved shirt. It was because my name was not only on his fingers, but also framed by the hearts that were tattooed on his arms.

The police came to our house one day to ask me if I knew anything about a boy who had been pushed through the butcher shop window and suspected that Ross had been the culprit. My mother became upset and probed me, curious if I knew about it. I grew worried that the incident may have happened because I had spoken to this boy and Ross may have become jealous of him, and the police thought the same. I was in big trouble at home because my mother was concerned that everyone in the street had seen the police cars come to our house; yet this wasn't the first time because on numerous occasions when my sister and I were little girls, the police had been called by neighbours when there was a 'production' in our house, and we were getting the *4x2*. Our house had been much quieter of late with my mother's new-found happiness, but now she told me I had embarrassed her as the entire street had seen the police come into our house, all because of the company I kept! My parents never knew about the happenings on the weekend they were away, but at the time I was sick with concern that the police may tell them.

I tried to put the past events behind me, and I only felt happy and unafraid when I was with my friends. Lucky for me, Ross was staying away these days and I had great relief when I heard that another girl was now going steady with him, which was probably why he was no longer hanging around my street. Previously, and quite directly, this girl had brashly told me that she would 'get him' and that she would be 'better for him'. Later, I heard she had another boyfriend whom she broke it off with in order to go steady with Ross.

In the sixties, there was often a police car just driving around the streets, looking for boys hanging about, and potential break-ins. Still an issue simmering in the background, every so often the police would stop their car to ask me with genuine concern how life was these days without Ross in it. One officer went as far as to tell me that it was a good thing that he now had another girlfriend because he would only get me into trouble, adding that my parents must be glad that he was now out of my life. A detective arrived at the house and took pleasure in telling me that Ross would be charged for pushing the boy through the butcher's shop window and furthermore, even though he was denying it, that they *knew* he did it. Someone had apparently witnessed the event. Charged, Ross was soon to go on trial. The police assured me that he would be locked up again.

Instead, Ross was released on bail and placed on a bond to attend court in a month's time for possible sentencing, along with advising him that he now needed to behave and to keep out of trouble. When I heard that he was away staying with a brother, which was a long way from home, I felt it would be safe for me to visit his mother and Tina. I told his mother about the time he had bashed me while trying to get more than a kiss from me. She was glad I hadn't told anyone else, and my skin prickled as I couldn't tell her that I already had. I felt like a different person these days, likely because I was hiding so much, feeling unable to tell anyone.

I heard that while Ross was on parole, he had to keep attending a job that he had in a paper factory. One day, thinking he was at that job, I again went to visit his mother and Tina because his mum was always happy to see me and I was able to talk to her about Ross, and Tina had become a friend of mine.

After a couple of hours, to my shock, Ross turned up

unexpectedly, whereupon an argument began between Ross and his mother. He was screaming loudly and upsetting her. I told him to leave her alone. Knowing he had to behave, I was no longer all that afraid of him, so I pushed him away from his mother. Being on parole, I thought he may be a bit fearful of doing anything wrong and he wouldn't physically push me around; I also thought about the night at home, which was now a few of months ago. Assuming he didn't know I had already told the police, I wondered what more he could do to me? I was worried that the police would bring the subject up with him — then he would know that I had told them!

I was wrong to think that he wouldn't hit me, as Ross hit me, and I fell back onto the grass. A neighbour hurried over to see if I was alright and offered me a lift home, telling me he had rung the police, but also that he wanted to get me home before they arrived.

I began to develop a black eye again, so over the next few days, I told everyone it happened from running into the clothesline at Ross' house, although I think those close to me were able to work out where my black eye really came from.

I was enjoying my new job in the newsagency gift store and presumably Ross was taking advice from the police and staying away from me. In a few months, I began seeing more of Frank, and we began going to the movies at the local drive-in. Sometimes Ruby and John came with us in Frank's car. We took other friends too, squashing them on the back floor of the car so that they didn't have to pay. There were some cars with younger ones together, including me, and cars with boys from the older crowd. We all parked close together along the back fence near the girls' toilets and the shop for our ice creams and chips at interval time. These were good days in my life with nice memories — going out with Frank felt right. Ross had been staying away, and I thought he was most likely enjoying time and events with his new girlfriend. I was relieved and glad about this.

A few weeks later, after one of my Physical Culture lessons in the new club, still wary of a potential visit, I hoped to get home one afternoon and escape Ross by walking behind the shops in the next street then up the track behind the garage where Jenny lived. Here, I could cut through the bush. I was always aware he may just be waiting at the end of my street and going that way would give me the benefit of seeing him first so that I could sneak around the other way and avoid him. Just before dark, I reached the bush track. Relieved he had not turned up; I also knew I would be home in twenty minutes and felt safe.

Halfway through the bush track, Ross appeared. He'd been waiting for me, and he grabbed me roughly, holding me captive in the bush. I was terrified when he told me that he'd heard I liked Frank. I don't know how he'd found out, nor did I know how he knew I would be sneaking through the bush. He told me he was afraid to be sent to prison for pushing the boy through the shop window, saying he would *never* have me if he did. He said he couldn't live without me, and he would rather just *die*! He was going to cut my throat and slit his wrists so that we would die together. Then, he said he would have me forever, because I belonged with him and *nobody* else could have me. Then he pulled a knife from inside his shirt! I was terrified and I began to cry when we both heard a man's voice coming from a window in a house nearby and echoing through the bush in the still afternoon breeze.

Ross grabbed me and held me tightly against him with an arm around me, and his other hand over my mouth telling me to *shut up*, then whispering again how sorry he was and how much he loved me, saying he didn't want anyone else to have me. I let him kiss me; I was terrified, trying to picture my surroundings. I could hear the creek water trickling nearby — I was planning my escape! I knew every bend, every rock and all the twists and turns in that creek from my many days running through there with Paul and Robbie.

We heard the man's voice again and it distracted him enough so that I was able to wriggle quickly out of his grip and jump over the creek to run home. When home, I burst into tears and told my mother, whose soothing words were that she had 'had enough' and did not want to hear about it.

Over the next two weeks, I stayed away from my Physical Culture classes and thankfully, Ross stayed away too, so I didn't see him for that time. He also didn't arrive at my work; I assumed it was because he was on a bond and waiting to attend court for possible sentencing. Things began to acquire

Chapter 5

an eerie feeling of peace, until a week later, once again, my life took another turn.

I was home sick with tonsillitis, and someone began knocking on the door. When he called out, I knew it was Ross. I didn't know that he had already been to my workplace looking for me and had been told I wasn't there, so came looking for me at home. I was too afraid to answer the door and was glad when he finally left.

I didn't know where he went until later that evening when my mother arrived home, telling me that he returned to the shopping mall to ask her where I was. She didn't know he had already been knocking on our door, so when she told him I was at home sick, he knew he'd been lied to, and decided to wait outside the shop where I worked just to make sure that I was not hiding from him in the back somewhere. When the shop was closed and locked, he walked to the little milk bar on the corner where I would sometimes meet the girls on their way home from work in the city and we would catch up on each other's news.

The following day, my friends related the events that happened when he arrived. Ross was looking for me and became furious when nobody could tell him where I was — nobody knew. Soon he was arguing with my friends and somehow got it into his head that I was hiding behind the counter and barged his way there to see. The man working there asked him to get out, but of course, Ross wouldn't, so the man approached him with the intent of making him do so. A bad move on his behalf because, apparently, Ross began grabbing goods from the counter and throwing them! Amongst many, he smashed a big jar of Easter eggs and grabbed the man, punching and struggling so fiercely that during the struggle, he bit a big part of the man's earlobe off! The police were called.

When my mother arrived home, she was furious, saying that this time she had really had enough. Though she didn't know the details of the events in the milk bar, she knew that with the police soon attending, Ross was involved. She informed me that she was too humiliated to return to work the next day. Apparently, I had embarrassed her enough, and she most likely would lose her job because of me! She said everyone in the shopping mall would know about this ruckus Ross had created because of the sirens from police and ambulance.

Needless to say, two days later when my sickness had passed, and on my return to work, I was sacked from the newsagency. Ross was soon in court and given a eighteen-month sentence, and again, I hoped at last to now have a normal life without trouble in it. Fortunately for me, my friends were able to help me get a job in the factory on the way into the city where they had all been working for quite some time.

With the shadow of Ross not looming over me, and now that I was working with friends, I was not afraid to be on the train any longer. Frank and I could also see more of each other, and six months later, we were going steady. After a few more months, I met his lovely mother, then, soon after, met his three brothers — one older and two younger — and a sister who was the youngest. Frank's father had passed away not long before we began to go out together, so I never met him. Frank told me his dad was a big drinker and very abusive to his mother, who was a softly spoken, gentle woman whom I never heard scream like *my* mother did. Nor did I hear any of his siblings giving cheek or having to speak loudly in order to be heard. *This was another normal family*, I thought, knowing that there were no 'productions' in this happy home! No doors being slammed or taken down.

I was enjoying going steady with Frank. I dreamed of having a happy marriage with him and having happy children. Because when I had kids, I knew they would be loved and never told to '*Get out*!' or threatened with 'turning ugly'. But for now, I was happy just enjoying my time with Frank.

This time Ross got 18 months sentence for pushing the boy through the shop window and other offences. Although he was given 18 months, he was out in 9 months for good behaviour.Quite by chance, a few months later I saw his new girlfriend on the railway station platform. She told me she was having a baby! When I told this news to Tina, she said that it was a lie. I told her that I felt Ross wanted that girl for what he couldn't get from me.

Even though I was aware that Ross was about, I felt

somewhat safe, and my relationship with Frank was lasting. On Sundays we'd all go to football to watch the local boys play League against other clubs. These were good days and I enjoyed being with Frank and the big crowd that we all hung around in. The boys in the football team all chose a nickname for themselves — usually a copy of their favourite player from the big-league team in the competition. Rugby League was a popular sport that most boys loved to play. We all enjoyed watching them play, especially now that some boys we knew were playing in the first-grade games that were heard on the radio.

The next biggest thing to happen in the shire was the new football oval and clubhouse being built at Cronulla for the Sutherland football team, to be soon relocated to Cronulla — now renamed Cronulla/Sutherland Sharks. This created a lot of interest around God's Country and local talent was sought after to play in this representative side.

These days, our local side is no longer comprised of local players, but players bought from all over the place. Rugby League is now a big business, but before this, many of the boys we knew were selected from the local teams and much interest came with the introduction of the Sharks into the big league, bringing a community spirit with locals trying to make a name for themselves. We all wanted to know a Shark, and with teams being put together mostly from local boys, meant that most of us did! It was usually a Cronulla/Sutherland Shark player who would run along beside the garbage truck, pick up the rubbish bin, and empty it into the back of the moving truck. Hard work and considered good training — cardio and weight training together — so much different from the training and fitness methods of today!

Chapter 6

Ruby and John were now talking of marriage. Frank and I were still going steady, and at long last, Ross was staying away after being recently released from prison yet again. I was also now not afraid to travel on the train into the city, so I worked in the factory with Jenny and Ruby. I often stayed overnight at Ruby's since the episode in the milk bar when my mother told me on more than one occasion to get out, not caring where I went. I hated being at home and hated looking at the broken door, which was a constant reminder of that dreadful night. When I stayed at Ruby's place, we all hoped Ross was too afraid of the police to come looking for me. He surely knew the police were just waiting to pounce on him for doing something wrong.

One day after leaving Ruby's, I went home to find a written message from Tina in my room, attached to a letter from Ross' mum asking me to go and see her. I felt that she cared more about what happened to me than my own mother did, so I went to see her. She told me that she wanted me to feel safe, so I was welcome to go and stay with her eldest daughter who was living a long way from there. She was married with three children and if I chose to stay there, I may be protected from Ross because she and Ross didn't talk. He knew the suburb she lived in but didn't know the exact location of her house, having never been there. When I told my mother, she said I should just go and not cause her any more heartache. My father showed more concern though, saying my life was safe only when Ross was in prison, and I should tell the police if ever I saw him again. At that time, I didn't know where he was.

A few days later, I told the police where I was going and they told me of their relief that I was able to get away from our house and hopefully, be in a safe place; further stating that Ross was 'not the full quid' and they were concerned about my welfare and safety. They considered him to be dangerous so when I explained that his mother suggesting I go to stay at his sister's and my mother saying she didn't want any more drama, the police agreed that this was a good idea. I was glad that they would know where I was.

Sadly, for safety, I then had to leave my job in the factory where the girls had been able to get me work. The following week, I was at Ross' sister's house, at last and finally, feeling safe. All was good except for being cut off from a life at home; I was close to my friends.

Ten days later, however, that feeling changed when Ross turned up, and strangely he was now a red-head! Unsuccessful at trying to go blonde, he had some success in finding out I was at his sister's house and where it was ...

When his sister told him to go, he insisted on staying and I saw then why he didn't get along with his family. He had his wrists bandaged after slashing them and told me he didn't want to live because I was now going steady with Frank. Perhaps it was that she felt sorry for him, or that it was less trouble for him to stay, but they eventually agreed.

On that first night he was there, he got into my bed and tried to have sex with me — I had never done sex (willingly!) and I was scared of him since the night in the room when he smashed the glass door. So, on this night, while he began to climb on top of me, I bashed on the wall to wake his sister or brother-in-law to come in. Sadly, it had no effect, and nobody came to my rescue. I was relieved when he stopped, and I told his sister about it the next day. The next night when he tried to do it again, I frantically bashed on the wall and this time, his brother-in-law heard and came into the room. I felt huge embarrassment because his brother-in-law saw what Ross was trying to do and he roughly pulled Ross off me. Soon, they were punching each other and suddenly Ross pulled a knife from somewhere. His sister threatened to call the police and Ross became quiet and cried, saying he would leave, but only if I went with him. Far too scared of him, I just couldn't and was relieved when his brother-in-law told me that I wasn't to go with Ross. Ross stuck to his story, but Ross' sister and brother-in-law weren't buying his behaviour, and after a little while he threatened to kill himself. Seeing that he wasn't going to get any sympathy, he then, much to my relief, took off.

Still shaken, the next day I was having coffee at a neighbour's place with his sister when we saw the police arrive. We both went back to the house, where the police began asking about the previous night. They told me that they knew all about Ross from talking to the detectives at the police station near my parent's house; also, that they were my friends and that I was not to be afraid to go with them to the local police station to make a statement about the previous night's events. Asking first, they then searched the house and of course didn't find him; no one knew where he had gone.

After I gave my statement, the police organised a lift back to Sutherland police station, which was closer to home. On arrival, the Sutherland officers then drove me home, and feeling safer, I told them of the last few day's events up to the night before. They were very good to me, and when home, they came inside to speak to my parents. They told them of their concerns that Ross may hurt me because he was unpredictable, and they knew that he now carried a knife. They told my parents I needed to be somewhere safe and well away from places known to him. During the conversation, they hadn't told my parents about the night the door was broken, for which I was so grateful.

My mother's reaction was to discuss putting me in a home for uncontrollable children, but my father approached a couple who lived on the other side of the highway. My mother knew the lady, because she worked in a little shop nearby and her husband was known to my father, having met while fishing. My father asked if I could stay there for a while and so it was that I stayed there for six weeks, *safe*. What irked me though was that once again, my life had been discussed without my input, almost as though I was a piece of furniture to be stored away for protection.

In a roundabout way, a calm and peace came over my parents' house when my father repaired the bedroom door that Ross had smashed. My mother never missing an opportunity to remind me how *I* was meant to repair it. Lucky for me, my father decided to repair it himself to keep the peace. I imagine that my parents were greatly relieved that I was away from them as it was unlikely that Ross would be coming anywhere near my parent's house.

I was visited weekly by the detectives at the nice couple's house where I was staying; they wanted to make sure that Ross had no idea where to find me, assuring me that it was in Ross' best interest to stay away from our house. Ross had sent Tina to Mum and Dad's house bringing mail, but my parents told her I'd gone to stay with my auntie in Newcastle, and they wouldn't be accepting any letters from Ross. My parents also informed the police of his sister's visit.

When the detectives came to see me, the head detective showed much concern, I think because he had a daughter the same age and he often spoke of her to me. I didn't know her as she went to the big Catholic school across from where I was now staying, and I didn't know anyone from there. Ross thankfully stayed away, likely afraid the police would pounce on him, and not wanting to extend his possible return to prison. Six weeks later, his court case was held.

I had not been out while staying with my parents' friends, in fear of being seen by anyone. My friends were all told I was at my auntie's place up near Newcastle and Tina relayed this to everyone. After Ross' case had been heard, the detectives came to tell me he had been given a hefty sentence and that it was now safe for me to return home.

When Ross was once again behind bars, it was safe for me to visit his mother, who was concerned about him being sent to an adult prison where there would be hardened criminals, afraid that he would be corrupted. I felt sad for her as I knew in my heart it was already too late for that. It was good for me to have some relief from him and his harassment, and I was pleased that each weekend I was now able to go to the football and watch Frank, where I could see Ruby and John.

I was horse riding on my own for much of the time because Kris was often grounded as her horse King often escaped his enclosure and did the rounds in the shire helping himself to neighbour's gardens, eating the yummy flowers. Robbie's mother's flowers were slowly diminishing because King ate all that he could, which got Kris into a lot of trouble because the flowers were Robbie's mother's income, supplying the florist shop that was joined to the funeral parlour. No flowers meant no income for her, and grounding was often the end result. In those days, there was always one of us grounded for one reason or another.

I am now going on seventeen and Ross at last is behind me; I am a working girl, adjusting to a now normal life. At last, there is peace in our house, and best of all — the butterflies I got in my tummy are not from fear of Ross, but joy each time I saw Frank, and for the first time in my life I can see how a nice boy treats a girl and I think I am falling in love. Frank was a gentleman, and with his soft nature and respect for people, I was very attracted to him. Also, it was nice to be treated well with no fear of a meltdown from him. I enjoyed his company and looked forward to seeing him each time.

We were spending a lot of time together and life was good. I wanted to be with Frank every spare minute. I had not felt like this before, so horse riding was not first on my list of priorities. With Ross back in prison, our house was a much calmer place, especially with my mother now being overjoyed since becoming a grandmother. As a direct result, we had an abundance of flowers growing in the gardens and I would imagine that my father's record collection had stopped shrinking.

Ross' sister often visited me, bringing letters from Ross for me to read, and although I liked Tina, I only wanted to be with Frank and didn't want to know what Ross was doing or how much he loved me and how long it would be before he was home.

Over the next year, Frank and I spent all our time together. My parents were very happy about this, and when Ruby and John were married, I knew, despite my parent's approval of Frank, marriage for me just now would be out of the question — there had been so much trouble and it seemed to still taint my life. The detectives would still often call in to ask how things were and how life was with Ross away. The head detective who had shown real concern told me his daughter had heard of Ross — well, the entire suburb had.

Ruby and John were married on a warm sunny Saturday afternoon in the little church near John's parents' home. Ruby's father was so happy for her, showing much approval of John with a warm welcome to the family in his speech ... Frank was groomsman, and I was bridesmaid for our best friends. I didn't have a good going-out dress because mostly my clothing outside of work consisted of jeans, slacks, and some T-shirts. I was able to borrow a green dress from Kris because her mother was a dressmaker, so Kris had a few dresses to choose from. I can't recall ever owning a dress — the closest thing I had were a few work skirts. My mother was proud to become involved in the wedding plans by being able to supply a lovely bunch of flowers from our now flourishing garden, which had since ceased to be pulled out by the roots after an altercation.

We had a lovely night with the reception at a local restaurant that was very popular in the sixties. I began dreaming of marriage to Frank. I knew better than anyone that Frank was the best thing that had happened to me, treating me with respect and always considerate. This was a good change for me, and I truly appreciated him. Frank had a good job, and this was another thing that impressed my father, who also enjoyed some male company. During his conversations with Frank, Dad talked about his fishing expeditions at Port Stephens where we spent many school holidays and he would fish for marlin and jewfish, sometimes catching a shark. These fishing trips were with my uncle and another mate who had his own television quiz show. I think Frank may have been a little bored though when my father showed him his darkroom that he built to develop his own photographs.

Home was a nice quiet place until a year later when I discovered I was pregnant, and things went back to being crazy in the house with my mother screaming furiously and telling me I was not to keep this baby and it would be adopted out. At the time, I was hurt how she was so angry with me after things had been so good of late and found it hard to speak to her for fear of more arguments. Frank, although overjoyed at becoming a father, was young and a little nervous. He didn't want to disrespect my parents, perhaps thinking that he'd disappointed them, and my home was not the nicest place to be for Frank, even for tentative visits.

I was confused over how much Mum loved my sister's son but did not want me to have this child. My father said

Chapter 6

it was because my sister had done things right by getting married first and my mother was probably just embarrassed, wondering what our relations and the people in the street would think. I suspect that at the heart of it was that I was doing most of the cooking and housework still, and it would have been a big thing for Mum to lose. This was also in light of all the unwanted attention of the past few years when Ross had been making a nuisance of himself — at our house, at the shops, at my job, and even in the train station when I travelled home from work.

Despite all of the ongoing tension in our house, in February 1968, I was overjoyed to give birth to a baby girl, and excited how my mother was able to come into the labour ward as my first visitor. I was so very, very happy and knew that I would love my daughter in the way I had wanted my mother to love me. I would understand her needs and be the best mother possible.

Frank visited and was overjoyed at his little baby girl; however, in those days there was a stigma attached to having a baby out of wedlock and the situation was still difficult. We were happy though. He tended to avoid visiting often, I think wishing to avoid a confrontation with Mum.

My happy world was soon shattered a couple of days later while in hospital, when a lady came to visit me. I didn't know her, but she quickly let me know she was from the welfare with papers for me to sign — adoption papers. She told me that after speaking with my mother, both of them had come to the agreement that my baby would be adopted out. She also told me that my baby would be best with someone who was able to give her everything I couldn't. *What about true mother's love? Nobody could love her like I do!* To this very day I have never forgotten that woman's name.

I began to get physically sick when she put the papers in front of me, forcing the pen in my hand saying I *had* to sign. I felt betrayed by my family as she told me the decision had been made and that now, they only needed my cooperation. Worse — if I didn't sign, it really didn't matter, because since I wasn't married, the appropriate people could just take my baby, therefore I had no rights, so I should just sign. She told me she was doing this for me. It was a common happening in the sixties — some babies were just taken. With her insisting I sign, and with me being so upset, the lady in the next bed left the room to get a nurse to ask this horrible lady to leave because I was crying and began being sick. As the lady from the welfare left, she turned to me and said that the appropriate people would be coming to see me. *Who was appropriate?* I wondered. I thought she was a *bitch* and most likely had no kids of her own.

After this visit, I wanted to leave, but in those days a stay of at least five days in hospital was required and I had such a terrible, long birth with complications, and had only been in for three days. A matron or head nurse had tried to make me breastfeed by forcing my baby onto me, but I had no milk, which in hindsight was probably due to stress. Cruelly, she told me I was a hopeless mother who couldn't even feed her own baby. This hurt me very much, but I couldn't help it if my milk never came, I didn't know why but I see now that I was emotionally burnt out at eighteen.

That night when it was dark and the other women in the room were sleeping, I began thinking about the lady from welfare and the things she had said to me, on top of what the matron had said, and I became afraid that my baby would be taken from the nursery while I slept. So, I crept to the nursery and wrapped my little girl in a bunny rug — somehow, I remember to this day how it had little pink and blue bunny rabbits on it. A nurse appeared and asked me what I thought I was doing. I began to cry and told her I was worried and had been told that someone could take my baby because I wasn't married. I asked if I could stay in the nursery until morning, but although she said no, she was nice and calmed me by assuring me that she wouldn't let anyone take my baby. On my return to the bed in the ward I was still unable to sleep. I had been in hospital for four days.

When morning came, I was spoken to by a doctor who said someone would ring my parents' neighbour to ask my father to come and take me and my baby home. Soon, my father arrived, and I was back at my parents' home, where to my complete surprise, my mother was showing a gentler side.

To this very day, I think my father had a talk to her because she was much softer when I returned home. My father called my baby Leigh, his little princess, and my mother began making little things for her. Three weeks later, Ruby had a little girl, and our daughters have very similar names. My mother became a loving grandmother to Ruby's baby also, making matching bonnets for our little girls. Whatever she made for my baby, she also made for Ruby's baby, and I saw the softness in my mother that I had craved when I was little.

Becoming a grandmother again was the making of my mother, who became the world's greatest nanna, even though I was so hurt that my mother had sold my horse while I had been in hospital. My father told me to just let it go because I wouldn't have time to go horse riding now, and it was one or the other.

Frank and I were still seeing each other — both being so young and with a baby, there was still much to sort through. Interestingly, my parents never dictated terms to me, or told me I was not to see Frank. Ruby and I were happy mothers and we both had many admirers at the football on Sundays. With all the things being needed to take along with babies, each Sunday at the footy was like packing to go on holidays. My mother made matching bottle warmers, bibs and bonnets.

Life was good, especially now with the relief of Ross being away and unable to upset my life and everyone in it. My father told me that my little girl should not be christened, saying: 'People are no better because they are christened', reminding me that I had never been christened. He'd also say: 'christened men created world wars'. I was beginning to understand why my sister and I were never allowed to attend scripture classes or even mention the name 'God' in our house, so Leigh was not christened.

One Saturday afternoon, a man came to the house, asking for me by name. I didn't know him, but when I went to the door, he told me he had been in prison with Ross who would be out soon and was going to come and pay me back for not waiting for him. I abruptly closed the door in his face, quite rattled, but soon forgot the incident. I should have taken more notice ...

At home, things had been calmer, and I was happy that relations seemed to have improved with Mum, who enjoyed making lots of little things for our babies. Life was the best that it had been for quite some time. I was so happy to be a mum and now, again getting along well with my mother. And so it was that a year later, she suggested that she'd mind my daughter for three days a week when I was offered casual hours back in the factory where Jenny and a lot of my friends worked.

My sister had moved out and was now living in a unit at Cronulla. She was working, and her son attended the same school that we had gone to as little girls, which was close to my parents' house. So, my mother minded him after school and I saw a beautiful warm, new woman in her, filled with so much love for her grandchildren. We were getting along like a couple of girlfriends, and it was now more so that my sister had differences with her, although I felt bad about all the trauma my teen years brought to Mum's life.

There were many occasions when I wanted to cuddle up

to my mother, feeling that perhaps she wouldn't push me away as she had when I was a little girl — and yet my arms refused to work. I was happy though to see the love that Mum showered on Leigh, even though initially she said she was to never come into her house. Mum had truly softened into a wonderful nanna. While she may have not been the most loving mother, she has made up for it by becoming the world's greatest grandmother.

Tina still brought letters to me from Ross in prison. He wrote that he was happy I was with Frank because I deserved someone good like Frank, so when I thought of the visitor's warning that Ross was coming to pay me back for not waiting, I was more concerned about the change in attitude from him, not about the threat. A few months after this, I heard that Ross was out of prison; I was surprised he had not been to visit me, yet relieved to have not seen him.

A few weeks later on a Saturday afternoon, I walked to the corner to use the public phone, leaving my daughter sleeping in the house with my mother, who was baking biscuits. I don't know why, but while I dialled the number, I turned and saw Ross driving past in his brother's car. I had a sick feeling that something was very wrong and ran home to find my mother in a state of terror, screaming! Neighbours were running towards our house to find out what was wrong. While my mother had been occupied in the kitchen, Ross had gone into our house and taken my daughter out of her cot as she slept.

He had woken her, and she was now screaming; he had a knife to her throat as he took her out to the car and left. *MY GOD! That's when I saw him drive past!* Something had made me turn and look, just at the time he drove by — *was it instinct that had come over me I wonder?* One of the neighbours went to call the police and another was calming my mother, while yet another offered to drive me to his house. On the way as we went past the railway station, I noticed the car again and we could see that a crowd was forming, and something was happening at the station.

    We stopped and I ran onto the station and froze when I saw Ross with my little girl, agitated; he was threatening to jump in front of the next train! A stationmaster had called the police and we heard sirens approaching. Ross hurriedly gave my baby to a couple of girls who were on the station's platform, then he ran away. The police arrived, I was given my baby, and they took the two girls to the police station for a statement. My neighbour was asked to take me there to also make a statement and I realised that I should have taken the threat much more seriously. It seemed that my life had taken a back flip and that there may be some troubles returning ...

Chapter 7

Ross was charged with attempted kidnap, but with a good solicitor, he received only eighteen months detention. My father was furious, because Ross' broken parole conditions had only added a further few months. My comfort came from the police, who called to our house every few weeks to see how I was and if I had heard from him. They told my parents of their concerns that I could be in real danger on Ross' release. My father didn't hold back and told them how let down he felt by the legal system.

Ross was released in nine months on good behaviour. Lucky for me, he did not come near, though he sent via his sister many letters of love and apology asking to be my friend, telling me he still loved me and that he wanted me to be happy, saying that Frank would be good to me, but wouldn't love me as he did. Ross knew that the police would be watching closely, just waiting to grab him if he again violated his parole conditions.

When the police called in to see me, my mother didn't mind so much because they were detectives, and as such, respected members of the community. In her naivety, Mum thought our neighbours were unaware it was the police who visited, as they'd always arrive in unmarked cars. The police comforted us by saying that if anyone was watching our house for Ross, he would also not suspect they were police cars. Little did Mum know that most of the neighbours already had a good idea of what was going on. The detective who had shown much concern for me also wanted to see any mail I had received. Obeying the conditions of his parole soon became too much for Ross.

In the sixties, many hotels had a band playing, mostly for free. We only had to turn up to see popular bands. Some bands, like the Bee Gees — who we were now hearing on the radio — had left Australia for overseas, hoping to crack the big time and potentially make a name for themselves, which the Bee Gees did. We also saw Australian bands like The Easybeats, ACDC and The Angels to name only a few, and many solo artists like John Farnham. One night, my mother was babysitting because we had all been invited to a local hotel to celebrate one of the boys turning twenty-one. Most likely, he was also one of the few who was legally old enough to be in the hotel. Most of us were asked by the doorman how old we were, we would just say eighteen, and in those days that was enough.

Boys used to think it wasn't cool to dance, so the girls danced together on the dance floor. On this particular night, we were enjoying our dancing when one of the boys rushed towards me and grabbed me, pulling me off the dance floor. Worried for my safety, he told me that Ross was in the hotel, drunk and calling out for me. This boy pulled me out into the car park and took me between two cars, telling me, 'Don't move no matter what!' He knew Ross very well and what he was capable of because he only lived three houses away from him, so I took notice of his warning and stayed there, terrified of what may have been happening.

I heard sirens and could see blue flashes. Half an hour later when it became quiet, one of the girls came out to get me, telling me it was now safe. Ross had been seen crossing the street, so he had gone. Then, as we walked back inside the hotel, there were more flashing lights, red this time; somebody yelled out that this was an ambulance. I didn't know what had happened and I began crying and thinking, *Oh God, please don't let him be hit while crossing the road!* At the same time as fear was coursing through my body, I realised the strangeness of me having any concern for Ross' welfare, given all that had occurred. Then one of the boys came out with his girlfriend to get me and we all left. I had wanted to stay at the hotel when the ambulance came, in case Ross had been hurt, but I couldn't tell this to anyone because nobody would ever have understood. *How could I expect anyone else to understand when I was unable to myself?*

As we left, I noticed there seemed to be a disturbance of some sort going on at the front of the hotel with most of the patrons now going out to the street. Weirdly, I again wanted to stay to make sure that Ross was not hurt. There were more sirens and I saw red flashes of light from another ambulance being reflected on the buildings. I was feeling sick, praying Ross hadn't been hit because someone said that they last saw him crossing the road, which only confirmed and increased my earlier fears. Unable to find the words to explain, I left with my friends and went home.

Tina visited the following morning asking me had I heard the news on the radio about Ross. Looking for his girlfriend (*that would be me,* I thought to myself) and unable to find her, he had left the hotel, and as he did so, heard some people across the road at the taxi rank who were just waiting for a taxi and having a few laughs after a night out. Their laughter got Ross thinking that they were hiding me, so he crossed the road, smashed his bottle of beer on a pole and thrust it into the throat of one of the boys who was laughing.

One of the girls at the rank was a nurse, so she was able to apply pressure to help ease the bleeding until the paramedics arrived. I heard that this helped to save the boy's life. I am sorry it happened to this poor boy, and over the years I have felt responsible. I am glad Ross never found me on that night because I may have ended up being the victim of his drunken rage. *Oh my god, when will this end?* I wondered anxiously. Ross was on the run again ...

A few days later, the police came to our house to ask if I had heard from Ross. I didn't tell them at first, but I'd received another letter from him via his sister. Tina had told me that their mother was sick and wanted to see me, but I was afraid to go to the house in case he was waiting. I didn't go to see her, and this saddened me because I liked her and felt sorry for her. Ross went into hiding.

I will never know why, but I wanted him to get away. At the time, and many times over the years, I thought of my reactions and wondered why a small part of me had considered his safety. *Was I afraid of him?* Over the next few weeks, the police visited on numerous occasions, Mum still blithely unaware that the neighbours had made their own assumptions about what was going on. Detectives repeatedly asked if I had heard from Ross. In the beginning, I didn't tell them about any letters I had received from him via Tina. I later felt I should, so I told them, remembering how they had been so good to me previously when I needed their help. Now it was they who needed my help; they were wanting me to set him up and get him caught before he hurt anyone else. In his letters, Ross had been asking me to meet him, insisting that I not discuss this with anyone at all (but I did tell Ruby). The police told me to answer him when I received the next letter, which would come sooner or later via Tina. I was not to go looking for her but just wait, and in a fortnight, she arrived with a letter in which he told me that he was hiding and asked would I meet him just a few train stops away from where I lived. I agreed and asked Tina to pass it on to Ross. It was arranged that in a few days Tina would let me know

Chapter 7

the time in the afternoon and on what day we would meet ... I was scared! The police told me I would be safe because they would protect me from Ross, who had soon planned a time for me to be there. I asked the police if Ruby could come with me; they agreed, knowing that Ross would be aware I wouldn't go alone. A plan was set to catch him.

Ruby and I got off the train, nervous energy making us walk quickly in the cool night air to the corner where Ross had asked me to meet him. The police were close by in an unmarked car, looking just as they had described they would — like people waiting for a rail commuter. When Ross arrived, he looked and seemed okay and he smiled back at me at first, so we approached him. Suddenly he turned and ran away. He suspected something was wrong! Was it because Ruby was with me? Did he intend to hurt me? Try to take me away?

When Ross ran and jumped into the bushes near the railway, the police allowed him to escape, later telling me they suspected this was likely going to be the case. An attempt to capture him might have placed me in danger, they explained, also pointing out that it was only a matter of time before he would contact me again. They were right, and a new plan had to be made.

Before much longer, Ross made new arrangements, this time our meeting was to be four stops from Sutherland, and in a laneway close to the station. In case the reason for Ross' previous flight was due to baulking at seeing Ruby, I went alone. After telling me that officers would be travelling in the same carriage, the police then instructed me that if I saw them, I was 'under no circumstances to make any contact with either of them'. The plan was for me to act normally, and when I got off the train I was to go straight up to Ross and be myself. Ask him why he ran. Ask him anything! 'Just act normal,' I was told.

When I got on the train at 7.15 pm on Sutherland railway station, I saw the policeman and policewoman in plain clothes waiting at the end of the platform to get into the same carriage as me. They smiled at me. As asked, I looked away and didn't speak to them. Because one of the police was a female, I felt safe. I found a seat and sat stiffly until the train left and reached Mortdale, the station where we were to meet.

Although the police had explained about there being laneways that were in the plan, I wished I'd listened a little harder as I found myself faced with a few lanes to go down. I couldn't see Ross, but I did see someone sleeping in front of a shop. I never found out if that person was drunk or an undercover policeman. Had I gone to the wrong lane? Maybe Ross was in the other laneway! Feeling at the mercy of a plan that simply had to go right, I was about to backtrack when a I heard Ross calling me. I quietly followed the sound and found him at the end of the laneway where I let him hold my hand. When he attempted to kiss me, the police came out of nowhere and grabbed him. Another grabbed me and took me to a waiting car. I felt awful. I cried to have done this to

Ross because he was screaming out for me to tell them that we had a date! But I was scared of him, now knowing what he was capable of doing. He hadn't changed his ways and I was afraid it was only a matter of time before he hurt me again.

Ross kept screaming, saying we needed to be together, but they handcuffed him and took him to another car. As I travelled home in the police car, his screams and pleadings for me to go with him; that he *needed* me, echoed through my mind. I had sported a black eye on more than one occasion, and I felt he didn't mean to hurt me, but just had no control over his emotions. Somehow, I cared for him, but I kept that to myself. What if the police were right and he was really dangerous?

Almost as a bystander from afar, I heard the police outline to my parents the problem of how Ross' infatuation with me would likely become increasingly problematic. He was very unpredictable and unstable, they urged.

Sometime later, Ross was sentenced to five years in prison for slashing the man's throat and a further two years for breaking parole and other offences. I wondered when I heard the news if NOW, just maybe, my life could be normal?

Chapter 8

Still in prison, Ross wrote me letters asking for my forgiveness. He'd tell me about his counselling sessions, which were an attempt to help control his emotions. He still asked if we could be friends when his time was done. For the first time in years, I was enjoying my life, now with the freedom that I had previously not had.

Not before time, things around our house (and in my life) were becoming peaceful; my mother was much calmer, so we were getting along well. I was loving being a mother, and so was Ruby. My mother was becoming a new woman, and I think it was such a shame that we had so many bad days when I was getting into trouble with Ross. (Later years saw her being very different, and we got along like a couple of best friends. On reflection, I am sad that my youth brought along so much drama for us all.)

Frank was terribly upset with Ross' behaviour and the thought of what could have happened to our beautiful baby girl. It took quite a while for things to settle down with him, which it eventually did. I was loving my times with Frank, knowing he was not about to be attacked by Ross, and eighteen months later, I married the love of my life, Frank, in the little church on the grounds where my sister and I had learned Physical Culture. My father, the atheist who had sworn *never* to enter a church, walked me down the aisle, and his presence in church must have been accepted by the powers-that-be because the church is still standing to this day ... My parents could not have been happier, and neither could I. We had a small reception in a tent in my parents' backyard. The only thing that disappointed me was that Ruby was unable to be part of my bridal party because she was due to give birth to their second child any day. My sister and 'always-in-trouble' Jenny were my bridesmaids. Ruby's husband John was partner to Jenny, and Frank's eldest brother was my sister's partner.

My mother invited a lot of people who I didn't know to our wedding. I suppose she was pleased that things were going well, and so proud to bring Frank into the family. After our wedding, we rented a little unit in Cronulla and now, when I look back, I can see that it was the happiest I had ever been; having a man who really cared about me and a child whom I was so in love with and eager to raise with love and understanding.

After two years, I became pregnant with our second child, and Leigh, at two and a half was eager for the arrival of a brother or sister. With a real knowledge of what was about to happen, she was quite a conversationalist. Ruby had child number two a little after our wedding — a little boy, and I hoped I would also have a boy for Frank.

While I was pregnant, I started minding a baby boy for a girl who lived upstairs. She seemed to be at a loss with motherhood, not knowing how to calm her baby, and had no idea how to lull him off to sleep. I became her mentor; I had a certain 'touch' with babies, and I enjoyed helping her and became very attached to her little boy. I wished she would just leave him with me because she had no idea how to nurture him, and I would almost cry for him when she brought him to me each morning with a wet nappy, wearing only a singlet with spew on it. I wanted to keep him and make him safe. I was so attached to him.

One morning, she almost belted my door in, bashing so hard. I opened the door and saw the desperate condition she was in. I ran upstairs with her and found Billy dead in his cot. She told me she couldn't stop him screaming the night before so had put him in his cot with his bottle in his mouth, propped up by a pillow so he wouldn't lose it. Sadly, Billy had choked on it. I was terribly upset and asked her why she hadn't come for me. I would have helped her with him. This poor little three-month-old boy.

I have heard it said that God takes first, those he loves the most. Maybe if there is a god then he was taken to be in a better place? Thinking like that brought some balance for me. That day, Frank stayed home from work to be with me because I was so upset.

A week after that terrible shock, and five months pregnant, I began to lose blood. I was afraid I was going to lose my baby. Frank and I were both saddened by past events, and it was now such a sad place to live, so after the bleeding had settled down, we moved to the other side of Cronulla. I didn't keep in touch with Billy's mother, and now I don't even recall her name. I never wanted to see her again.

A few months later, after a somewhat touchy pregnancy with shows throughout, I gave birth to my second child, another little girl whom we named Maria. I was pleased to have given birth to a healthy baby after the upsetting time in my pregnancy.

Three years later, when Leigh began school, we moved back closer to my parents' house and Mum once again was a big help at that time, minding Maria three days a week. I returned to work again to help save money to buy our own house. My mother and I were growing closer, spending a lot of time together — in fact, I don't know how I would have worked without her help. I fell pregnant with baby number three two years later. I was pleased that everything was moving along just as I wanted, because I wanted lots of kids with Frank.

My life and Ruby's were quite similar, with Ruby just having baby number three. Another boy, so surely I would also have a boy this time. My tummy grew huge, and I was told at six months the reason for this ... twins! Now, just maybe one of them will be a boy, I thought.

I was unable to do much with constant pain in my lower back from a kidney infection that seemed to clear up only to return with a vengeance. I was constantly short of breath, and with the back pain, Frank did most of the household chores. When I reached six and a half months, I woke one morning in extreme pain, and I knew it was more than infection. Frank rushed me to the hospital while I was experiencing labour contractions that I could not hold back. It seemed my twins had decided to come into the world early. Still having eleven weeks of pregnancy to build my babies, I didn't want to have them so early for fear of losing my precious little gifts but was unable to prevent labour.

At hospital, I was told my babies may die if they were born now because it was too early. But what could I do? I tried to hold them back but couldn't. First born was a little girl, followed in six minutes by a little boy! Finally, a son for Frank! But both were rushed away from me to be placed into humidicrib for special care. Not prepared for such a thing, Frank and I cried. Our excitement was now replaced with the terrible fear that our little babies may die.

The following day a priest arrived, asking if we would like him to christen our babies. NO! To have this done would be like admitting defeat. I told him that they would survive, and I would have all my children christened together. At the time it didn't enter my mind that he may have been a little curious about my answer — him a man of God and me not having been allowed to have any faith. After two days in hospital, my little boy, Raymond, was transferred to the Prince of Wales Hospital for specialist care and placed on a machine that would breathe for him. His little lungs were underdeveloped and not strong enough to distribute the various gases in the oxygen that he was given.

I wondered what I had done that was so bad to deserve this and many questions whirled in my mind. Was I really *so* bad? Is that why all this has happened? Was I being punished? What has Frank done? What has our little boy done? He hasn't been here long enough to do wrong! Why was he struggling just to breathe? I remembered my mother often telling me that bad things would happen to me because I had hurt her so much, and I assumed that it was actually happening. But why hurt my little boy? He had done nothing wrong, and to add further horror he had also developed cystic fibrosis. Our little girl, Joanne, could stay in the humidicrib for specialist care, but I was advised to return home, the staff explaining that it was best for my other daughters and for me to be at home. Frank could bring me to hospital whenever I wanted, and that way I could visit both babies in both hospitals.

I returned home, but felt I was deserting Joanne by leaving her in the hospital. I ached trying to find strength, although I knew she had to stay there for care. I was fretting to bring her home with me, but I also needed to be with Frank and my other little girls.

Each day, Frank and I would go to visit Joanne, and in the afternoon, I would go with my father to the Prince of Wales to visit my son. I was heartbroken, because I was only allowed to look into my son's crib. I wanted desperately to hold him close, but I couldn't touch him. I could see his little chest working hard, heaving in and out, each breath for this dear little life a massive job. I hated to see all of the tubes coming from his little body and I had to accept that these tubes were doing a job — keeping him alive. I was so sad to not be allowed to hold him for concern of cross-contamination, which I didn't understand, and I told them I didn't have any germs — 'I am his mum; he grew inside me'. I desperately needed to hold him close to me. I had an ache in my heart to hold him. I wanted to feel his breath on my cheek; I needed to smell him but looking was all I was allowed to do. I began to send all of my mental energy into the crib to give him the strength he needed to survive. On those days, my father came the nearest to praying I ever saw from him, looking at my son, saying he wished all his own strength could be transferred to my son's little body. I knew what he meant. Sometimes he would talk to the universe and ask for help for this little boy to survive. Isn't that a kind of praying? He would say all this while holding the side of the crib, his eyes full of tears, not allowing any to drop. Most days on the way home I could hear him sniffle back his tears.

 I had seen my father cry many times when I was a little girl while he was putting soothing balm on my wounds, inflicted from the beltings he had given. I had also seen him cry when he had been in an argument with my mother or while she was screaming at him and smashing his records. But I had never seen him so withdrawn, showing such concern. I knew these were different tears, not from anger or remorse but coming now from concern and an ache for my hurt. Seeing my hurt made him ache in the way only a parent can ache when their child is in pain. My father, who had belted my sister and me, leaving huge marks on our bodies, warned by police to stop belting us, was now reduced to tears when looking at my son. I began to realise the many emotions he had carried within, and I was learning the many sides of emotions, recalling how he convinced my mother to let me stay at home when she was telling me to get out of her house and go to live in the gutter, 'where I belonged'. When she wanted to send me away, it was he who found me somewhere safe to live with his friends for protection. His softness was now being expressed and I recognised the difference between physical pain and emotional pain. I was now so much more aware of my father's carriage of such torment within, and how my mother's yelling was all too much for him to cope with on top of his other pain inside.

A few weeks later, Frank and I survived Christmas in a blur, pretending to be happy for our other two girls. I remember it was emotionally very hard and I began to detest the carols playing everywhere. I hated seeing everyone being so happy while my world was falling apart. On New Year's Eve at eight in the evening a phone call came that changed my life.

Our little boy had stopped breathing and had given up on his fight to stay alive. He was too tired to fight and keep on going with this battle that had been put on him. I began asking myself, why couldn't I have kept him inside for a few more weeks? Couldn't I do *anything* right?

Frank and I sat quiet for a long time. I don't have any idea how long, I just know it was a long time; we sat, we didn't talk, unable to make any sense of this little boy being given such a short life, suffering, only to be taken from us. I loved him and still, to this day, I feel love for him. I remember the feeling of desperately wanting to nurse him, to hold him close to me. I remember the sadness and pain inside, the aching in my heart and the sickness in my stomach. I wished it were possible to write a letter to God who I also was now beginning to doubt. I wanted answers! What had happened in our lives to deserve this loss we were now feeling? Why this? Why that? Did I not look after myself while pregnant?

In a few days, we had a funeral service for our little son Raymond. His little pale-blue coffin is forever etched in my memory. His ashes have remained with me because I believe that his place is with me — his mummy. I talk to him, knowing he is here with me and not somewhere else. I didn't want him to be in the cemetery where he could be feeling lost and alone, or afraid to be away from family or from me. Here with me is where he belongs, safe in my love and always with me. Frank and I agreed with each other that whoever of us died first would take our baby's ashes to heaven with them.

Chapter 8

I doubted that two little children would scout around and put flowers on graves as Robbie and I had done in years gone by.

These days, when Christmas carols with their jolly expectations of happiness and joy to the world ignite inside me, they bring sad memories to the surface, reminding me of those days. The horrible aching that was topped with awkwardness, knowing that people didn't know how to speak to either of us, and probably felt wrong or guilty in their excitement of Christmas approaching. I felt like my heart had been pulled out of my chest and I am now, truly aware of another emotion — a mother's deep aching heart pain.

Part of me died on that night.

In the past when I had been hurt, it was different to this feeling of being broken. I had carried excitement in the previous six months, knowing I had a good chance to have a son for Frank. I was numb with grief, carrying sadness and a curiosity that continued to make me wonder if this was what my mother had meant when she had told me that I would be hurt one day? For a long time, I ached, wondering that if there is a god. Why put my 'badness' on a dear little baby who had done no wrong? Why give this little child sickness? to teach him to fight? To then abruptly take him away? Is my father right and there really is no god?

This event in my life not only turned my world upside down, but also brought with it a distinct feeling of division — the time before my twins were born and the time after. Both times felt like two different lives. Before — a life full of expectation and excitement, carrying those babies with the possibility that one would be a boy and a dream come true for Frank. Then, the life after they were born, which featured days turning into weeks of fear and the questions within, followed by massive disappointment and heart pain with the questions — Why did this happen? Was I being punished for something I had done? Did I not take enough care of myself while carrying the babies? Was it all a consequence? I had been raised with consequences, now I was carrying so much pain and confusion, and I angrily asking why. I ached, constantly thinking how much I had wanted to hold him in my arms but wasn't allowed to touch him because of cross-contamination. Dear God, I was his *mother*; he had grown inside of me. I felt cheated by not being allowed to hold him close to me and now he was gone. I thought how I never held his little body close to mine, I never smelt him, never felt his breaths on my face and I loved him so much. The days following his death I was in no condition to look for answers, so I made them up; coming to the conclusion that it must have happened because I had done something *very* wrong back when my mother and I were fighting every day, and now I was truly feeling the results of consequences. As far as my mother was concerned, the reality was that I should try to get over it because I had other children who needed a stable and calm mother.

    I didn't know anyone who had something like this happen

to them so there was nobody I could talk to about the pain I was carrying in my heart. Nobody raised the topic with me; I assume because none of the people in my life knew how to talk about it and comfort me. I think most of my friends and family thought it was too painful for me to speak of my loss and they were right. I never spoke of it to anyone and yet, today, I am fully aware that I should have done just that. Frank and I ached for so long, carrying great hurt inside, and we learned to bear the feeling of unbearable loss. Somewhere in my heart I believe my baby boy was aware that he was very much loved; after all, he heard every heartbeat of mine, and he knew I was his mummy.

I can see the destruction this bought into in my life. Now, the only thing that pushed me forward was my precious little surviving twin and my other little girls at home. I have a knowing that my baby boy was aware how much he was loved. He will always be with me; this I know because I carry him in my heart. Sometimes I spend days with him constantly on my mind. If I were to pull a positive from this event I would ask, did it happen to make me become stronger and wiser? I learned how time does not *always* heal but can teach us resilience and endurance.

As much as I love Christmas with its twinkling lights and happy children, I can no longer listen to carols ... *Silent Night, Holy Night ... Sleep in Heavenly Peace.*

Chapter 9

While my son had teetered on the edge of life and death, I felt my father yearned to do something good, but he was in such distrust of God that he was only able to wish, not to pray. Sadly, during this time, I didn't see any real concern coming from my mother. I didn't want to think badly of her, so I reminded myself how she had never given me love or expressed real concern over the dramas in my life so why did I think this time was any different and that she may show some? I was learning that she was unable to express love in a nurturing capacity. Now, I was just glad we had become closer in the past few years. She had been always on hand to mind my other daughters when I had needed to go to visit either twin in hospital and was a very good nanna, spoiling my girls at times. But she never seemed to realise how *I* needed some love and comfort from her too. Her support for me consisted of telling me to stop crying because it wasn't good for my girls to see, and that I needed to be a calm mother to my baby girl who would be soon coming home; I should pull myself together. Although her idea of support was to stop me crying, I badly needed to cry, couldn't she see that? She could advise by using strong words, but Mum was unable to comfort me in a loving, motherly way, seemingly unaware of my need for a cuddle from her. I wanted her to show some concern. Even if she had gone to look at either one of my twins, it would have been something, but she never did. My mother is not a hard woman, yet I didn't know why she never went to see my babies, and later, I wished I had never asked her ...

After my son died, I was now able to stand up to her without fear, or care of being told I was cheeky and 'turning ugly' because of speaking up; no longer afraid to be punished by her. One day, I asked her why she hadn't visited my babies — her reply was that she was too busy. This is not the mother I later became so much closer to, so perhaps I'll never know what she was about in those dark days. I began holding back my feelings from her with the promise to myself to be a better mother for my girls and to *always* express love and concern, and hopefully, give good advice when needed. I began to stay away from her house because I was hurting whenever I went there, so my visits were less frequent.

A week before Easter, my little Joanne was brought home from hospital. Dad had retained his interest in photography and asked me if he could visit a lot so he could take photographs. I agreed, so there were many taken of this precious little life now four months old and looking more like a newborn every day. Easter arrived and with it came and the famous Royal Easter Show. On Good Friday, Ruby and I went to visit my parents, and my father suggested Ruby and I take our eldest girls, now both aged around four and a half to the show, suggesting I buy a Cadbury chocolate showbag for my mother, who was in need of some sweetening up (according to him). My mother never realised that my father meant well but he had the personality of a mischievous little boy. She always took him so seriously and this would upset him when she became irate and slammed the doors.

Around that time, my father had been experiencing an emotional breakdown and over a period of a month he had been sent home from work on two occasions with sickness. One day when Ruby and I were visiting, he was laughing and telling us about his sleeps at work that nobody was aware of until the day before, when he had been found sleeping in one of the buses that he was meant to be working on. He had been suffering with chest pain and sent home. With Ruby and me, he seemed well and happy, and laughing like I hadn't seen him laugh in a long time. After my son died, my father seemed to lose some sparkle. It was good to see him back to his cheeky self, even though my mother was a little disgusted at his corny jokes. Little wonder he felt that she needed some sweetening up.

Frank was a good daddy and entrusted with the care of Marie and Joanne, so Ruby and I were able to go to the show for a couple of hours, which was better than good medicine for me and just what I needed. We all had fun on most of the rides. I purchased a Cadbury chocolate show bag for my mother and a Sambo Liquorice show bag for my father.

The next day, Palm Sunday, Frank drove me to my parents' house with the sample bags, dropping me at their front gate with the intention of picking me up in a few hours. In the sixties and early seventies, most people burnt their own rubbish, and my father was an early riser, burning rubbish early before any neighbours would hang their washing out on the Hills Hoist for drying. This Sunday was no different to any other Sunday, but I couldn't see him in the yard burning off as he always was. I let myself in the back door. My parents had not been sleeping together because my father had become very restless and was keeping Mum awake, so he'd been sleeping in the room my sister and I shared as little girls. When I let myself in, I saw my mother not long out of bed, sitting at the table having her toast and marmalade, unconcerned that Dad was still in bed at nine-thirty. I was shocked because that was not like him, so I opened the bedroom door. I then knew why he had not risen — he wasn't breathing. My father was grey. He was dead. Having seen death before when I had to say goodbye to my nanna, I remembered that awful colour.

Unable to hold me up, my legs gave way and I dropped to the floor. When I was able to get up a few minutes later, I ran to the neighbour's house to phone for an ambulance. The neighbour then drove me home to get Frank, and on arrival I told him about my dreadful discovery. We returned to my parents' house just as the paramedics were taking my father out on a stretcher to be taken to hospital. I don't know where my head was, but I asked, 'Do you think you can revive him?' Another neighbour had gone to my sister's place on the other side of the railway to tell her about it.

I have often thought how strange it was that my father, who didn't want a thing to do with God, died on such a holy day as Palm Sunday. I am grateful that Ruby was still close to me when I needed her in my life at that time. Ruby and John's move away to the central coast was not until the following month after the birth of their third child — another boy. My parents had both organised many months prior to have their bodies donated to the medical university when they died and so it was that this was where my father spent the next eighteen months before Frank and I were able to pick up his ashes to place him in the ocean where he had found the solace that he loved so much. This is where he wanted to be when he died.

In the weeks and months that followed, I became very distant from my mother and sister, and a few months later, Frank and I moved to Queensland for a new beginning, but our stay there was short, mainly because I was missing my friends, needing them so much, and yes, to my surprise, I was actually missing my mother. My life with Frank had changed so much and was vastly different after all of this heartbreak. I felt that my life had been divided, again, and there was a distinct before and after, like two different lives.

Chapter 9

Frank had a good job in Queensland and was doing well in his new job with new workmates. I was alone with my girls a lot and became homesick and wanted to return home. So, in a few months we returned to Sydney.

My mother and sister had become closer, now going out together to the local clubs to dance whenever possible. Over the coming years, my mother became very well-known by the locals on her nights out dancing. Her stamina surprised many people who would see her dancing until late on most weekend nights. Jenny was going out to the clubs with them, often laughing when telling everyone how my mother was able to out-dance her. And not only that, my mother was always the one being asked up for a dance by obliging men.

When Frank and I returned home from Queensland, we rented a little house near his mother's place, but I became a bit like my mother, slipping in and out of moods and slamming doors. Luckily, Frank didn't take the doors off like my father had done with ours! After a few months, I began working a casual job doing an afternoon shift, which meant I could still be with my girls as much as possible. When my mother decided to sell the family house, the benefit of my working paid off, because Frank and I had saved enough money to be able to buy the house.

After Frank and I had bought the house, my mother moved to Cronulla, close to the beach that she and my father loved. The little cubby underneath my childhood house was still intact, although it had none of the homely decorations that

I had furnished it with. I was happy that my own daughters could play in it now and I hoped that they didn't need to use it as an escape from me.

Frank and I had both changed, still coming to terms with all the events of the past. I had now become quite an impulsive person and Frank was a drinker, staying out late on most nights. Both of us were carrying too much hurt from the loss of our son and coping in ways that the other wasn't able to understand, which caused many arguments. It wasn't only us; so many things had changed, and sadly, Ruby and John had parted, so it felt like nothing was the same. To make things even worse, being impulsive, I was not thinking in a sensible way, and I bought a dog. A big dog — a huge Great Dane.

I intended to enter Bailey into dog shows and win, so I put much effort into training him, which gave me something outside of my home to focus on. Needing to be trained well, I spent all my spare time show training him in the park at the top of our street where we had spent many bonfire nights when I was a little girl. Soon I was winning many shows, which were precursors needed to qualify for entry into the Royal Easter Show; the show that everyone tried to enter and win. I continued training every chance until he was perfectly trained, and I soon qualified for entrance. My determination to be the best along with my constant training and coaching paid off by the fact that he gained first prize. After that day, he went on to win again, this time against other dogs who had also won their class. I had achieved my dream!

Chapter 9

I was still having occasional emotional blowouts, always feeling bugged, not knowing it was an anxiety thing. I didn't try to repair it and have since realised I should have had grief counselling after our son died, because after that time, a huge change came over me. I became a different person, feeling I had let Frank down and blaming myself when he was frequently out at the hotel drinking. Now I see that this was his way of coping, easing his own pain and feelings of loss. I didn't realise it at the time, because I was too young and emotionally torn, and had no knowledge of the different ways we all cope with grief. I became introverted, wrapped up in my own feelings, shutting down from Frank — no wonder he stayed out. I don't think he would have enjoyed being at home with me, particularly when I was a crazy person who had taken my grief to a depth that changed me. I blamed myself for our loss, feeling I could do nothing right.

My mother was unable to comfort in a loving capacity — I don't think she knew how to. As a child, she was unable to give me the love I craved, and now I had become like her, slamming doors and occasionally throwing things. I had issues that I didn't understand and my anger and hurt consumed me, so in hindsight, I would have most definitely benefited from counselling. But I wasn't 'nuts' — a person only had counselling if they were 'nuts' — I was just hurting, and so sad … My weight plummeted to a tiny six and half stone and my heart often pounded so much that I was becoming breathless.

My blood pressure would also skyrocket. A rush visit to the doctor found that I had a goitre from an overactive thyroid, and I needed immediate surgery to avoid permanent damage. I was glad to have a reason for my moods, outside of emotions, because I thought I was just becoming like my mother — putting on a 'production' with my emotional outbursts.

I tried to become pregnant to have more children, but I was confused as to why I seemed unable to fall pregnant, especially since I had never taken birth control pills. Surgery on my thyroid went ahead and I recovered well, gaining weight immediately, and was told that I could easily fall pregnant now. The doctors were right because I became pregnant very soon after. I was also told I should be careful to not get pre-eclampsia again and I discovered that it had been the culprit for my twins' early arrival. For five years I had blamed myself for losing my little boy, thinking I hadn't taken good care of myself while pregnant, only to find out now I wasn't actually to blame for the early arrival of my babies. So many questions coursed through my brain, like why had no doctor told me I had it and what it was? If I had known, I may have been able to avoid the early delivery or possibly the doctors didn't know I had pre-eclampsia until after my babies were born.

Our first Christmas in the house brought a mixture of feelings with a mixed bag of memories of my own childhood. I recall a realisation of doing all I could so that my girls would have a better time growing up than I had experienced in this house, and I *knew* I could make that happen. I would make sure they were happier than I had been. Being pregnant again pleased me because I had always wanted many children with Frank. The following year on January 28th I gave birth to another girl — Raelene. Over the years, I self-consoled with thoughts that my little boy had gone to heaven to make way for my fourth daughter. I now believe that all things happen just as they are meant to and at the right time. I didn't understand or like that consequence then or now, but I needed to accept that things happen that way.

Our girls were all attending the same school that my sister and I had gone to, each doing well in all subjects. I was very conscious of not making them feel they couldn't be themselves. I allowed them to express their opinions without the threat of becoming 'ugly'. I tried to channel their strengths in order to not break their spirit, and when they fought with each other, as sisters of their age do, I would tell them: 'You should fight FOR each other not WITH each other!' I didn't want them fighting like my sister and I had done.

In the following years as my girls grew up, I was happy that my relationship with my mother had improved and I shared my daughters with her, knowing this was what she needed, and she loved them very much. She minded each of them so I could return to work, so I made myself let go of past hurt from her. On my days off, we spent many days together at the beach in the rock pool called the Nuns' Pool, named so by the locals on account of being overlooked by the nursing home built on the promenade in Cronulla, which was run by nuns. My sister was able to get me a job working some afternoons as a waitress and bar attendant in a local club where she worked. The girls grew very close to my mother. I was sometimes asked to work nights, and she was happy to mind my girls, giving her the company that she needed. Mum usually looked after them at her place in Cronulla, but she sometimes she slept over at our place. While minding the girls, she would teach them how to make little gifts, so there were always little token gifts of love waiting for me when I got home. My mother often called my girls her little beach babies.

In those days I saw the love my mother was able to give to my girls who truly adored her. I wanted to cuddle her and tell her 'I love you', but I was unable to show her any love with any physical embrace. I bristled and it always hurt how she didn't seem to care for me when I had needed her support over the years when Ross had been stalking me. She never knew of the terrible night with Ross and the true way that the bedroom door was broken — I didn't care what she thought and yet I had told her I smashed it. Even after the detectives told her my life was in danger, support or understanding was non-existent; she didn't seem to care saying of me: 'Well, there's a gutter out there, she can go and sleep in that!' Even many years later she was still unaware of the drama in that room.

When I had wanted to put my arms around her, they wouldn't respond, but I was happy to see the love she gave to my daughters and the love that each of them returned to her.

When they spent time with her, this made her very happy. Sadly though, I had become emotionally stunted and unable to embrace her. On the days with her at the Nuns' Pool, I was pleased how she had mellowed, and I found comfort in telling myself that if I wanted to see her show love and affection to anyone, it would be to my daughters, so she was only doing that which I would have wished her to do. Each day at the beach was enjoyed with a picnic lunch of chicken sandwiches followed by homemade pikelets.

Most days, a lot of new friends — mothers who I had met through my girls at school — would come along with their daughters or sons to the beach, so my girls mostly had a friend from school with us. My mother was always dressed up to the nines, looking like a ten. Many people walking by would stop and say hello and commented on how lovely she looked, to which she would flash those eyes and say: 'Oh! Who me? Oh, thank you.' Then everyone would hear about this for the next few days as my mother loved a compliment and she seemed to thrive on the attention. No wonder she was called the 'lady on the chocolate box' — she was such a glamour!

Despite disturbances in our marriage since losing our little boy, our girls were doing well at school; so much better than I had been with my schoolwork. Though I excelled at all sports and the success had made me popular at school, topping all expectations and pleasing the teachers; academically, I was just an average achiever, not a student who gained A passes like my daughters. As a girl, because I had learned consequences, I was now trying to teach my girls to be good and wholesome. Leigh was a good student, gifted with a natural ability for drawing. Not a great deal like me in looks, she looked more like my sister and my sister's son. I always thank God she was not taken from me, like the babies who often were taken from unwedded mums in the sixties. I was never going to let that happen. My next daughter, Marie, was topping her class in all subjects; an intelligent and clever girl — of course, she had plenty of time for homework, not having to do housework outside of general chores like I did. Most days she was a little defiant, refusing to do homework, but fortunately she managed to top the class in most subjects, even going on to become Dux of the School. She took after me in the looks department, yet her academic intelligence was acquired from her father.

Our twin, Joanne, was getting good marks in subjects, and I was told she was a busy talker in class, often organising others. Now a schoolteacher herself, I think she was born to teach, yet in class she had also been mischievous, having a personality similar to my father's — in her looks, she took after Frank's side of the family. Our youngest daughter Raelene, who was just in the early part of her school years, looked quite similar to my mother and a little like me, and she excelled in all sports as I had done.

Sadly, Frank and I were soon having problems which we were unable to solve, and four years after our beloved Great Dane Bailey died, we separated. Frank began to write me many love letters, yet nothing changed my mind; I had been so unhappy, and we divorced a year later. The letters kept coming and today I have them in the suitcase with my special treasures. They have travelled up and down the coast with me on my many moves — house to house, state to state. After fourteen years of a marriage, which I had wanted to last forever, the remnants now remain under my bed with my school reports, trophies, medals and certificates from Physical Culture, my sporting events, dog shows, and other achievements. Numerous little gifts of love made by my girls take pride of place in the suitcase, as do each of my daughter's special achievement awards. Not only had my life changed significantly after the breakdown of our marriage, but now our daughter's lives were also affected by this awful twist.

After Frank and I parted, my mother often stayed overnight to mind our youngest daughter, now aged eight. A good deal older at thirteen, fifteen and seventeen, sometimes the other girls would go to Frank's for the night. I thought often about Frank and the damage to our marriage that I had allowed to seep in from past events. I was sad on realising I had allowed these events to dissolve our marriage instead of making us stronger together. I will always remember the softness and good within Frank, the love of my life, and how I loved him so much.

I was working in the club bistro where my sister had arranged a job and out of the blue one day, I was told Ross was back. To my horror, he simply showed up one day much to my surprise. Clearly, he had asked around and managed to track me down. He stood there awkwardly not saying much. I asked him to please stay away saying I had little girls and that I didn't want them to see or experience any violence. I prayed desperately that he would stay away, and luckily, he did ... he unfortunately would come back into my life many years later.

While working in the bistro, I met Anne, who also worked there. She was good friends with my sister and soon she and I became good friends. When my mother was having a sleepover at my place, Anne and I went out dancing after work with other girls.

A couple of years later, I was pleased to hear that Ruby was returning from her move to Queensland, especially because I had missed our friendship. I was able to get her a job in the same club and at last, some part of my life had returned to a (nice) shade of my past. I was enjoying my job and loving the nights out dancing after work, knowing that my girls were safe with my mother or sometimes their father. Mum and my girls would make biscuits and small cakes, which we would take to the beach the next day. She taught them how to paint their fingernails and toenails; the importance of face crème; how to knit and sew; how to make paper flowers. Other lessons included how to answer irate people in order to escape them and how to pinch flowers from neighbouring gardens! They made many little handcrafted things, so I was always given a gift of love made for me during times spent

Chapter 9

with her. It it pleased me to see how wonderful she was for my girls, who all loved her, having a vastly different relationship with her than I ever did. They were all so happy to be with her. I wanted my girls to be trusted and respected, and I would often tell them of the importance of friendship, being there for friends, holding their secrets, and to consider friends as being someone worthy, especially including each other and themselves. I always remained loving to them so that each of them knew I loved them unconditionally.

Over the years, sometimes I have been called 'smother' instead of mother! Too many cuddles? I had become overprotective of my children, likely a result of Leigh's attempted kidnapping and it had stuck with me.

I wanted my children to stay strong for each other at all times and be able to vent their differences without arguments ensuing. My sister and I had fought all our lives because our mother had played us against each other, although I think that she was unaware of doing this. My sister and I only worked this out when we grew older.

Time marched on and it was now six years after my divorce with Frank. I was a little jealous hearing he had a girlfriend, but I realised that our lives were vastly different. Ruby, now back home from Queensland, found out that at thirty-five she was going to be a grandmother! I enjoyed rubbing it in that she was getting older now.

When I had been working in the bistro for almost three

years, I heard about a new hotel that needed staff, and when meeting the manager of this place at a function, I was offered a job in the bistro. Anne also got a job, then Ruby, so now the three of us worked in this refurbished hotel with a nightclub, which soon became the busiest place around.

After a year, I was able to learn how to work the bar and also some office duties, including payroll and cash balancing, so I was soon working in the office on paydays and the public bar on other days. Leigh was working in the large shopping complex close to where I was working, so she often called in to have lunch with me on the days I was doing the payroll and office duties, which had given me some leniency and free time to share with her. She was now eighteen and a spirited girl, determined and driven with confidence. All boundaries I had placed on her became her challenge, something to reverse test me on in her own way. She was not about to be controlled by anyone, nor was she ever. With a good soul, she could be very loving with much softness and warmth, and although not always the best behaved, she was not a bad girl — she was just strong-willed. I knew she would need that strength in life and wished *I* had that kind of strength when I was growing up. Her spirited nature would not be trampled on, nor would it see her confined regardless of the cost. She had always pushed the boundaries when trying to get her own way. Leigh had had the same boyfriend now for five years so when she came to have lunch with me one day with the added bonus of her news of being pregnant, I wasn't too surprised. I wasn't going to treat her the same way I had been treated, and even though she wasn't married, I told her I would stand by her and support her all the way — Leigh having never known about my battles to keep her.

Now I had to stop stirring Ruby about becoming a grandmother and getting old, because it was also happening to me. The similarities between Ruby and me as young mothers repeated itself, as history so often does, with Ruby's daughter having a girl, and nine months later, Leigh having a boy. I was so excited to welcome this dear little life into our broken-down family … I was so in love with him, feeling that my love for him was coming from a different place because my love as a mother comes from my heart and my head, but my love as a grandmother comes from deep in my belly. *How gorgeous he is,* I marvelled. *My gosh, I am only thirty-five and have become a grandmother!* Ruby's and my life seemed to be back on track with each other, and it pleased us to have more things in common again.

I was divorced for almost eight years when a man by the name of James was employed as a new manager at the hotel. Still doing payroll and office duties, James and I worked closely together on those days. Some nights I did bar work and when the hotel was closed, James enjoyed buying drinks for all the staff; he loved making people laugh and I needed to laugh, so it was a natural progression that I liked being around him. He was a charming man with a quick wit, and I was soon looking forward to seeing him at work, especially the nights

I worked in the bar because after work on these nights, all of the staff would go into the city for time out together. Hotels in the city were open until late then, so when my girls were at home with their nanna or at their dad's, Anne, Ruby and I, and other staff, along with James, would go into the city.

I enjoyed laughter in the company of James, and it was only a few months later that I began to gravitate towards him, unaware of the abyss I was allowing myself to fall into.

Chapter 10

Being paymistress, each Wednesday — pay day — I worked closely with James in the office. Other days, I worked in the public bar serving many local men who seemingly had nothing better to do than to drink. All of them with an opinion, they would rave about the changes around the place over the years. Then they'd start on politics, bringing arguments between themselves, which I very often had to defuse before it became physical. Hearing about the changes in both the hotel and the surrounding shire was interesting to me. Although only a fifteen-minute drive, the journey to and from the hotel was all new to me and was quite an experience.

At home, I was enjoying the independence of living with just my girls, and yet, deep down I was missing the family life of marriage. My new concern was that my girls would go astray, as I saw that kids from broken families sometimes did. Those days I had great help from my mother, who was always available to mind my girls. She no longer seemed to me the unfinished woman I once thought, and she often slept over when I was asked to work nights. My mother and I were good mates, laughing together a lot; she telling me to stop making her laugh or she'd wet herself again. Our time spent together was now good, especially since she no longer told me to be a certain type of person and had stopped telling me that I became ugly when I had an opinion. The constant should and should nots from my childhood were no longer an issue.

James and I grew closer, and after about a year or so we became a couple, sometime later moving into a rented house together. Sadly, my childhood home that Frank and I had bought was now sold and a thing of my past. At times I wondered how it all had happened. I enjoyed minding my little grandson each Monday on my day off, so that Leigh was able to return to work.

Another three years later, James and I left the hotel where we had met, and I began working in a little club not far away on the other side of the shops. We managed to get hold of an old club building after a friend mentioned that it had become vacant. Finding out who the new owner was, James approached him, asking about renting it so that we could start our own business. After getting the keys, the more we were there, the more we discovered that the entire place was in desperate need of repair and cleaning. The place was overrun with rats and the many traps that were set were carried away with rats in tow, some traps never to be found. We were still excited though, and after work each day I would pick up my girls from school, then travel back to our new venue to clean and repair. When night came, my girls slept there for a few hours on a lounge in the office. With the help of James' mother and father, we all did our share of decorating; working hard and for long hours to make it presentable. We painted, cleaned, wallpapered — we did everything! James' mother, who was a good sewer, made curtains and tablecloths, and did any other sewing that needed doing.

Tradesmen were employed and after a couple of months of very hard work, with the help of James' entire family, we finally had everything in compliance with council, and after only a few squabbles with them, we were able to trade. Opening firstly as a restaurant, we later expanded our licence to include entertainment, which was when we began to make some money. James' mother and father were good parents and they'd been in hospitality businesses all their married life. James, being the eldest of nine children, was respected and admired by all of his siblings, so when we opened, James' entire family were more than happy to work in it and help in any way possible. None were so proud as his father, who worked tirelessly, his mother also helping every way possible. Soon we were making many new friends whom we have remained friends with to this day. The prospects for our future were so exciting, and when we began to make some money, we were able to purchase our own house on the other side of the shire. Although it was a longer drive, which I didn't like, it was better than paying rent money.

Sadly, my desire to be with James, and the many long hours

worked in our business, had put a certain distance on my friendships with Anne and Ruby, who were now working together back in the club where I had met Anne. We spoke often on the phone, but we didn't see very much of each other. My mother was now only looking after my youngest daughter, Raelene, and as a result of spending many hours together, they developed a unique relationship. Joanne stayed at her dad's and the oldest girls, at nineteen and twenty-one, told me they were too old to be minded by their nanna!

One night, I received a phone call from Anne to tell me that Ruby had suffered a cerebral bleed and had been rushed to hospital; things were not good. Anne proceeded to tell me how these bleeds usually kill people. I knew this because my grandmother had died of this very thing, and I was consumed with fear of losing my friend of thirty years. I was sad that we hadn't been in touch for a few weeks, seeing it as my fault, being too busy and allowing our side-by-side friendship to suffer. This horrible thing had happened to my dear friend Ruby! Three years before this, the same thing had happened to my next-door neighbour Monique, and it had shut her down completely, making her a prisoner in her own body; she lost all her physical abilities and was unable to do anything. The poor woman was strapped into a wheelchair, unable even to speak. Monique couldn't scratch herself, or call for help when needed, so she was at the complete mercy of her carers. I spent many days crying for poor Monique, often thinking how degrading it was for her, and when I wanted

Chapter 10

to help her, I was told that she had proper medical assistance. I wondered why a thing like this should happen to her and I cried day after day for Monique. *If God is real, why does he allow things such as this to happen?* Now, it had happened to my dear friend, Ruby. Once again, I am talking to God, who I wonder about. *If you are truly there, please help my dearest friend Ruby ... please don't destroy her body like what has happened to Monique.*

The next morning when I visited Ruby in hospital, I was relieved to see her sitting up in bed and able to speak to me while waiting to be transferred to another hospital for specialist care. When I returned home after the visit, I began to read through my medical books, learning that all bleeds on the brain are damaging, some more than others, and depending on the location and size of the actual bleed, they are graded from one to ten. A bleed over four is normally fatal. The person is usually affected by a stroke following such a bleed and most likely, from this stroke, a part of the body will shut down, bringing with it residual and permanent damage. People can become wheelchair bound. Bodily functions such as walking, speaking, eyesight, and the ability to process thought logically can be distorted and ongoing. Poor Monique's body shut down after having a level three bleed close to the pituitary gland, and this, sadly, was followed by a few strokes causing much more damage. Luckily though, Ruby was fortunate not to have needed surgery because the bleeding in her head soon stopped and she was sent home a few days later. I thanked God for this! *Just maybe there is a God*, I thought, and perhaps he'd listened.

Ruby survived this ordeal and, all these years later, our friendship remains as strong as ever, but at the time it had actually been a wakeup call for me, now realising how completely immersed and lost in James' world I had become! I learned not to take *any* friendship for granted *ever* again. No matter what happened I would make time to contact my friends and not focus on my own life so much.

My sister had been dating a man for a year and a half and they had an engagement party at our newly decorated building. Soon to have a wedding, my sister asked me to be her bridesmaid; I wondered how I would get through this for her. I was concerned because James and I had been having heated words over my need for a commitment from him. But I began to see that the things James had told me about myself were not nice, each most likely providing reasons for him not marrying me. James had never been married and had no children, although he was very good to mine, seemingly happy to spend an evening with myself and my daughters, plus my grandson. However, soon James moved way up north to work in a hotel with the intent to purchase if possible. Sadly, I wondered if this was a way for him to escape from me. I no longer felt love from him and felt inferior when I was around other women who did seem to be important to their husbands or partners. I was curious as to why, unlike them, I wasn't. My need to be loved by James may have arisen from my childhood though, so I reminded myself many times that it wasn't James' fault that I had this need.

Our flourishing business was no substitute for the love and affection I missed from James. I soon realised that he was so focused on current business opportunities, that he was unaware of my needs. I began to feel neglected, thinking he didn't care enough to notice. He seemed so focused on current times that he felt no need to look into the future and I could see now we had become business partners, not emotional partners. My sister's fast-approaching wedding was a concern for me, but I was happy for her to have a man who loved her and wanted her to be his wife — how lovely for her! James returned home for the engagement party and was returning back north the next day. The same procedure occurred when the wedding came about. He seemed happy to be away from me so, I wondered — was he trying to leave me?

My girls were each growing into young ladies, and I felt proud of each of them. We spent quality time together until the following year when Leigh and my grandson moved to England, as her husband had joined an English league team. I missed her and her little boy, whom I had become very close to. Two years after their move to the other side of the world, Leigh gave birth to a little girl. I hoped one day to fly to England to see them and to meet my new granddaughter. And now, Marie was also having a baby and due any day now.

When the business up north which James wanted to buy was no longer available, he returned home, and we moved back into the shire. I was happy to be closer to my girls and friends. A month later, Marie had a little girl. I began to think James had very little conversation for me, and he became upset with me when I told him so. We argued over my need for a commitment, and I became emotionally wounded. At that time, we were looking to buy a house with in-law accommodation so that his mum and dad could live with us.

We eventually bought a house, nothing flash, but in all the houses we lived in, this was my favourite. A neat little house with easy-to-care-for gardens, it had a partially independent sleepout that may have been the original garage. The backyard was long with a good garden and a log cabin; there was a slippery dip and a set of swings, which was much enjoyed by my grandchildren. A second storey sat on top of the house which provided a compact fully self-contained unit, ideal for James' parents. Here, we all lived together happily, and those days became special times in my memory. I was very fond of James' parents, and we all got along well. James' father, also named James, gave himself the special job of making breakfast every Sunday and we all enjoyed his cooking. He made the most wonderful pot of tea, and I don't recall ever enjoying a cuppa so much! Seems the Irish have a knack for making a grand pot of tea. Those are good days for me to remember; my best times in a family that I wanted so much to be a real part of. I was, once again, witnessing how a *real* family works. I have great respect for James' parents, whose children all stuck together, caring so much for each other, even attending church together on Sundays. These were the best family days of my life, but short-lived, as a few months later, James' father was diagnosed with lung cancer. We were all so saddened by this awful news. Eighteen months later, he died; it was like losing my own father again because he had become a special person in my life. Once again, I wondered how God works.

Soon after this, James' mother moved in with her eldest daughter to help with grandchildren who were still little. I imagine it was a good distraction from her recent loss, especially now that James and I spent most of the day away at work in our business. We were all so upset and sad; we all ached deeply from it. Being needed by her daughter after such an event may have been a blessing for James' mother — I could well imagine how she would have felt better living with her daughter. I missed James' father, and I often visited his graveside to speak to him, telling him all the latest news in the family, believing he was able to hear me.

After this terrible loss, and still living in the house with James, Ruby planned her second wedding with Anne being her bridesmaid, as I was unable to be bridesmaid. Saddened after my sister's wedding when I began to feel James didn't love me, I was glad when the day was over. I never wanted to go through another event like that — beating myself up mentally throughout the entire reception, wondering why James didn't love me enough for marriage. I tried not to become cynical, but I kept wondering if he would ever see something nice about me or just keep telling me all about my bad parts. James now invited others to join us when we dined out for dinner, and I wondered if this was because he didn't have to speak to me. When he told me all the things wrong with me, I was able to see the reasons he did not want marriage and began to feel truly unloved by him. To add salt to my wounds, a few months later Anne told me she was also getting married. Then, soon after, Frank was set to marry his girlfriend, who he had been living with, and I had confused feelings about this as well. Our girls would be in the wedding party, so it seemed that everyone was getting married, except James and me.

Luckily, we were getting busy in our business; lunchtimes brought in many local businesspeople, so it was easy for me to be distracted from my personal sadness, by throwing myself again into work. We were making a lot of new friendships and it was soon evident that it was time to hire more staff. When interviewing bar attendants, I felt I should leave the loudness and night crowds to younger girls, while a more mature woman would suit our day trade better. So, I employed a woman more my age. Georgia and I soon became friends, to this day remaining best mates, so I am reminded again that God must exist because she was put into my life when my life needed a friend such as her.

My eldest daughter in England had her third child, another boy, and was about to return home, which pleased me very much because I felt lonely when I was with James, and to have Leigh and my grandkids back home seemed to be just what I needed. After their return, my first grandson attended school near our house. We all spent a lot of precious times together until two years later another move came when my daughter and son-in-law moved north to Toowoomba in Queensland as he got a job there. After they moved, I began to feel an emptiness, made worse when James became distant. Again, I wondered if his distance was due to my constant requests for commitment. I tried to move on, doing things that pleased me, while trying not to be so available for James, especially when he made me feel so unloved. I thought about leaving him, but knew I was not emotionally strong enough.

Over the following months, I began to acquire comfort from a glass of wine, which, extended over the next couple of years, became a daily bottle (or two). I chose to look for work elsewhere from our own business and this was like leaving James without actually leaving him. I found work in a nursing home — after all, this was where my real desire was. I had always wanted to be a nurse ... denied when I was young, then having my children at a very young age, I knew it was a bit late in my life to become a registered nurse, but also knew I *had* to make a change. After searching for work in a nursing home, the only position available was in the laundry. While it wasn't exactly a career, I hoped it may lead to something better. I was so happy to get a start there as the job made it possible to leave my position in our business. I also hoped by doing so, James might actually miss me at work or appreciate me a little more.

Working in the nursing home was the first time I felt I was where I was meant to be, and soon, I was doing a course in nursing. I was very happy, wondering why it had taken me so long to do something I had always wanted to do. Now that my girls were older, I had a lot more time on my hands, so in my desire to become a registered nurse, I was now able to do a lot of study, until the return of migraine headaches which I hadn't had for a long time.

Much more than headaches, this time they came back with a vengeance. So, I called them head pains, crippling head pains. Then the eyesight in my right eye began to fail. Thinking I may have been reading too much with study, I had my eyesight tested, thinking I now needed glasses. After testing, I was told I had excellent eyesight. Now I realised that the headaches weren't like a migraine; something about them was far worse. I assumed my headaches were hangovers from drinking every day because they were aching, thumping, and throbbing. I knew I had to stop drinking but I justified it by telling myself that it was an escape to shut out my unhappiness. I truly didn't care.

My mother was quickly ageing, and living in the next suburb, she relied on me for everyday care. This meant that on my way home from work each day, I called in to check on her, making sure she had a proper dinner ready and that she was drinking water. She was sometimes bewildered and confused due to her not using her bowels or urinating enough from not drinking water, which made her a little toxic. Mum was also getting many skin tears, which were taking so long to heal because she now also had cellulitis. She was often confused and unable to correctly administer her medications even though they were conveniently packed in a daily pack with each day and time clearly marked.

Some days I needed to shower her and change her bed linen. I didn't realise it at the time, but her need for me may have been a good thing — a distraction from my own unhappiness. After tending to my mother, it was home to do my own household chores, then to the club to meet James on his way home from work.

I had at last begun a nursing course. *Better late than never*, I thought, but Mum let me know in no uncertain terms that she was unhappy about me looking after the residents in the nursing home. She began to phone the matron every day for one reason or another, telling her I should be looking after her and not there looking after others. She was right, because with her lazy bowel and her urinary tract infections bringing much confusion to her already anxious thoughts, she now needed constant checking. I always prompted her to drink water, which would have prevented the problem because her ever-present UTI kept her in a toxic state, sending her a bit crazy, but she often told me that she would rather drink poison.

Before long, James went down the coast to another hotel and this time he was away for three to four nights each week. I felt sure he wanted to leave me but was unable to tell me. I was so alone each night and my girls suggested I get a dog for company.

I didn't want a dog! Eventually I got one from a friend of my youngest daughter and it seemed exactly what I needed in my loneliness. This beautiful creature was named Dudley; my gorgeous new family member who thought he was a human! He became the one thing that kept me grounded; his need for me with his unconditional love, brought happiness into my life. He became my salvation, and I enjoyed teaching him lessons and taking him for long walks, mostly to my mother's place.

A few months passed and my youngest daughter Raelene, at twenty-four, began planning a holiday overseas to attend the wedding of James' brother, who had gone to live in Ireland a few years prior. Without talking about it, we both knew that I would feel so alone when she went. This is my daughter who still lives with me and with whom I am very close, the one I spend most of my time with. I had Raelene in an attempt to save my marriage with Frank. I wished she wasn't going overseas because I knew I would miss her terribly, but I also knew not to tell her this, knowing it would only make her feel too guilty to go. Besides this, travelling would be good for her, and I didn't want her to travel with the knowledge that I was sad about it. All too soon she was gone; away for nine months. With Raelene overseas and James away for the best part of every week, I was so lonely, and Dudley became the friend whom I told all my news to.

Over the next few months, I had continuing terrible headaches and was unable to get relief with any medication.

Chapter 10

In the past when I had suffered the occasional migraine, my youngest daughter — Raelene — helped with support care for Mum, but sadly for me, she was now overseas, and my sister could only call in on her way home from work to see if she could do anything. She was only able to take our mother out to the movies weekly.

I was alone each night with James still often away and so the offshoot of this was my drinking and dancing, with Dudley for company. I was drinking more. Before too long, the pains in my head became unbelievingly bad. I was afraid these pains were something else because they were a pain worse than I had felt anywhere in my body. I had been to the doctor on many occasions, but nothing would ease the headaches. I had trouble speaking because it made too much noise and felt like a jackhammer in my head.

Almost at the end of my tether after a few really awful months, I sought help. I had numerous tests done, unfortunately with nothing wrong showing up. Sticking to my not-so-enjoyable lifestyle, I was now popping painkillers with the wine.

On the weekends, if James was home, we would go out to dinner and because James was a very social person, it meant there was always someone else coming with us. I began questioning myself about staying in a relationship while feeling so unloved and unhappy, though mentioning this to James brought accusations of picking a fight. I was having thoughts of putting an end to our relationship as I was becoming more and more aware that our needs and wants were vastly different. My drinking, crying, constant needs and feelings were things that annoyed him. So how could we get married while I irritated him so much?

In time, the pains in my head became crippling. Some mornings, they were too painful to lift my head off the pillow ... This meant that I was soon having time off work. My boss suggested that I put my mother in respite care, also telling me to take a week off for further tests and some rest.

For six months I had been taking strong pain medications, yet nothing eased the agony in my head. All the testing had been done — again and again and with no presenting problem, and no relief in sight. The pain became unbearable, now restricting my movement as well as my speech. Sometimes I'd hold my hands either side of my head and whisper so as not to aggravate the pain and vibrations inside.

In an attempt to keep my mother safe, I had taken her Valium away when I discovered that she was taking them for everything from her urinary tract infection to constipation. This would put her in an airy-fairy condition, which had caused her to faint a few times; only to turn it around and inform me that this was the very reason I should look after her. The Valium, combined with her somewhat toxic and delusional thought processes, placed her in an even more confused state of mind. I hated seeing this once-vibrant, happy-go-lucky woman now zonked out on the medications, so I removed them from her home and took them to mine ...

Chapter 10

Before much time had passed, I realised that I needed to get them out of *my* house because now it was *me* who could not be trusted with Valium — they had to go.

Each morning when I dragged myself out of bed to try to get ready for work, I'd find half-full bottles and broken glasses, vestiges from my drinking sessions the night before. A part of me didn't care, although I realised that in order to arrive at work each day in a normal state, I *must* stop drinking at night, also thinking that it may help ease my headaches. With my youngest daughter overseas, and James rarely there, I was so unhappy and in such great pain.

After a referral from my doctor, James' mother came with me while I had an x-ray and further scans to try to determine the reason for my dreadful head pain. Constantly throbbing, when I tried to sleep it was sharp and intense. I also experienced loud noises similar to a surf pounding with crashing waves and lots of gushing and swishing noises. Sharp ringing in my ears would be followed by loud tapping noises and I wondered what the *hell* was going on in there? In my attempt to kill the agony in my head and to mask the chronic pain, I began taking strong pain killers every hour, if I needed or them or not. Soon I was taking double doses every two hours. I told no one, fearing they would take the pills away from me. I was very dependent on these pain killers, losing myself in a web of fear, wondering if I was hooked. *No, I was not hooked like a junkie*, I began comforting myself. It was okay, I was just doing pain management I assured myself, but in reality, I was masking my problems to be able to get relief before the pain returned.

I was sick of it all and I prayed for the morning to arrive so that I could get up on my feet and be near another person in case something happened to me. I was afraid to be alone when each day seemed to bring a new horror — from blind spots in my now-swollen right eye, to a stiffness in my neck such that I was unable to turn my head, and I found driving my car very difficult.

After a while, James returned home expressly to sell our business.

He started a new job in a hotel near the city. Some nights he had to stay overnight, and occasionally I would stay there with him, relieved to not be home alone with my sore head. When my eyesight began to fade even more, I had further eye tests done, once again finding nothing. Considering I endured the head pains for almost ten months, I was fed up with myself and unable to function normally; speaking became almost impossible with whatever was going on inside my head, leaving me feeling like there was a loaded freight train in my head.

At around the nine-month mark and quite desperate by that time, I received a phone call from Raelene in Canada telling me she would be home the following month. I hadn't wanted to worry her while she was holidaying, so I didn't mention I'd had to leave work during the past week, nor the concern my boss showed earlier, telling me to take time off, and to get better. Naturally, I didn't tell her about being unable to move properly, which had caused much pain and difficulty when trying to shower residents. With restricted movement from my stiff neck and failing eyesight, I then suffered repeated bouts of shingles on my lower back. Subsequently, I had no choice other than to leave my job.

The following month I was excited with Raelene's return home. She had been able to get her old job back. When I had told her of my debilitating headaches that were the reason for me leaving my job, she once again was able to help me with my mother who was needing a lot of assistance. Working in the city, my sister was unable to get flexible time and my other daughters were in jobs that didn't allow them to have the freedom that Raelene had in hers; Joanne was a schoolteacher and Marie ran a successful business from her home.

On Raelene's first Friday back at her job, she was able to take some time off work to come and meet me and help toilet my mother. Because of my condition, I needed assistance with my mother who had recently had a fall at home and was now waiting on surgery for a cracked hip. So, she hung onto me to walk, which pulled on my stiff neck and caused my head to throb loudly. I was jolted with every step taken. The gushing noises inside my head were frightening me. I was exhausted carting her around on my arm with this huge freight train in my head.

Chapter 11

In my loneliness, I payed music, drank (many drinks) usually to the point of being drunk, and I danced. Having a little party on my own, I told Dudles all about my sadness. Poor Dudley heard all about my hurt and feelings of no love from James. At work, or when I was out, I tried hiding my unhappiness from others, but I knew I was beginning to spiral out of control. I didn't care.

After calling into Mum's place daily, I'd then go home to take Dudley for his walk and training session in the park. Soon he was a well-trained, happy dog with a tail that never stopped wagging. Once trained, and a little calmer, I was able to take him to work in the nursing home on the days I did laundry.

Dudley enjoyed coming with me to work where all the residents remembered his name. I found dementia an amazing ailment with its long- and short-term memory loss. The ladies were often unable to remember their own family members' names, yet they remembered Dudley's every day, calling him over for a pat. He loved all the attention! Most of the residents suffered from dementia, yet when I danced with them each day before I left for home, they remembered all the words to the old songs. I also knew most of the words to the old songs because I had danced to some of them in a concert performance when I was a little girl. I loved working at the nursing home, enjoying the cuddles that each resident would give me. I wondered if I was filling a void from my early childhood. I didn't allow myself to focus on the negatives in my life nor carry sadness with me, knowing that I had a responsibility to myself to be a happy person. I enjoyed my new job and enjoyed learning about nursing. For the first time in a long time, I felt pleased to mean something to someone.

Some of the residents were quite quirky, and I loved the oddness in them. I occasionally set them up in a conversation, knowing it would bring about a crazy chat, which entertained us both with the most amazingly exaggerated conversations. Dancing with them brought some funny singalongs — my feet were constantly trodden on — with songs bellowed out loudly in my ear. If I danced during the day, Matron would remind me that I had a job to do, and dancing with the residents was not one of them, yet I continued to dance with them every day, and soon they began to expect it from me. Some even asked: 'When is it music and dance time?' Perhaps seeing the benefits, Matron relented, and over time we became good friends, remaining close to this day. When my daily job in the laundry was done, I danced before I left to visit my mother, who was continuing to phone Matron, many times daily. I could tell she was very jealous, and she was now becoming very naughty, playing tricks on me in her attempt to move in with me, knowing that James' mother had moved away to be with her daughter.

James and I bought another house close to where we had lived previously. It had a pool and nice gardens, which was very pleasing to me. In the work arena, I was doing my first aid and nursing certificates. Sadly though, soon after achieving my certificates, the nursing home was set to be sold. All the girls I worked with were saddened, as was I, and the residents, who were aware of events, were very distraught. Not really knowing exactly what was happening, some of the residents behaved like naughty children when they felt something was not quite right anymore. After it was sold, I was able to get a job in another nursing home and with my certificate for nursing under my belt, it meant no laundry — just nursing. This nursing home was located close to my childhood home (which I later bought). It was built over the creek where I swam with Robbie and Paul, and leeches, tortoises, tadpoles and who knows what else!

I enjoyed working in this new nursing home, doing many courses while employed there. I planned to enrol for more courses when the headaches I was still experiencing had left me.

From one resident's room, I looked out of a window onto the creek, with a good view of the waterfall and the pond under it. This opened many memories of my younger years, running through the drains and swimming.

Chapter 11

I still called into my mother's place on the way home, now growing concerned with her rapid ageing, along with ongoing and new developing health issues. Most days I needed to change her bed linen and saw to it that she had a decent meal for dinner, and she had used her bowels — in the toilet! I had stopped working Fridays in order to take her to the hairdresser for her usual comb up. This has been routine for her as far back as I can remember and she absolutely *had* to have her hair combed up every Friday — rain, hail or shine.

Once a year I drove north to visit my daughter Leigh and her family in Toowoomba. Before I left, I firstly organised my mother's week, including transport for Fridays to keep the routine of going to the hairdresser, so that she would remain happy. I knew my sister would call in on her way home from work every second day, but this wouldn't be until early in the evening, so among other things, I organised visits from her cousin, her friends and neighbours, and the local chemist to make sure she was taking her medications correctly. Even though they were packed in blister packs for each day, she would sometimes take two lots instead of one. Most importantly, it was vital that she was using her bowels so she would remain lucid; my mother needed a lot of care those days. Yet when in need of attention, she was still able to perform a dramatic 'production'. On my return home from Toowoomba, I would hear how hard it had been for her with me away. My sister had called in every second night on her way home from work but working long hours meant she was time poor. However, our mother loved that my sister was able to take her to the movies on Mondays.

When Mum was unable to get me on the phone — for any reason she was able to conjure — she would phone for an ambulance to take her to hospital. This happened on more than one occasion, and I felt that she tried to control my time with guilt trips; in fact, she would still have liked to control my life! This became obvious to me, as each time I went to her calls for assistance with the television remote, or a wandering spider that was gone by the time I arrived, she was packed, ready to come home with me for a few days saying, 'I'm all ready! *Oh gosh, my poor mother!* I couldn't have her stay because I was unable to leave her in the house to go to work the next day — our house had polished floors and a very large staircase. I was convinced she would take herself up the stairs and that she could fall down them. I was also concerned of a slip on our polished floors. Apart from all the danger in our home, if I am to be honest, I didn't want to put myself out for her, remembering my teenage years when she wasn't able to care for me and wanted me out. I helped her because I loved her regardless, and I remember how good she was and such a big help when my girls were little, making it possible for me to return to work. We had become much closer then, spending many days together at the Nuns' Pool or the local swimming baths.

Now, her need for me was a good distraction from my own unhappiness. I thought I was in control of my emotions;

however, when I wanted to embrace her, I couldn't. Was this a hang-up carried from when I was a little girl in need of her love; a time when she seemed to have had such great ability to love other neighbours' kids, yet not me? My sister has since told me that she had felt the same denial from our mother.

These days, I remind myself I am a mature woman, so I ask myself: *Am I just getting in my own way?*

Frustrated with the noises between my ears and the loss of eyesight, I was also totally pissed off with my mother, who said that she would rather run naked through the shops than have me put her in a wheelchair, and if I did put her in a chair, she would come back one day to haunt me!

The shingles on my lower back returned every three months and was not only painful, but also made me sick in the tummy; so, on top of everything else, I was sick and tired of myself. I wanted to be anywhere but taking my mother shopping and to the hairdresser.

One day, Raelene met us for lunch, and to help toilet my mother, but she soon realised she had to rush back to work. Ominously, I called her back for a goodbye kiss as I like the proper farewell. As it happens, we were then all unaware of what was happening inside my head; none of us were prepared for such an event, one that would turn our world upside down and place me in the fight of my life, changing my future (and the beginning of these pages).

I am glad I was unaware of what was happening. The last thing I can recall is running into a friend after lunch, who said, 'Oh my god — you look awful!'

I told her about the pain in my head, explaining that it felt like a huge, loaded freight train and a semi-trailer together, yet ... like an aching numbness ...

I can't take it anymore ... I want to rip my head off!

Chapter 12

Oh shit, when did I put myself to bed? I don't remember! How come I don't remember? That's not like me. I'm unable to get anything to trigger the chain of events necessary for me to get into bed! I can hear beeping noises now I'm awake — my eyes open and I look around ... *SHIT*! This is not my bed! I am in a hospital and the beeping noise is coming from a machine beside my bed. What has happened?

I had no idea (at that stage) that I had been in a coma for two months, on life support with a tracheotomy to assist my breathing. I was unaware of how long I had been there. I began to think about my mother. Where is she? Has there been a car accident I don't remember? Have I killed her in a car accident that I don't remember? I began to throw my legs around to make sure that they are still attached and working. I tried to call out to her, but my voice wasn't coming out. *Shit*, I don't have a voice! What is wrong? Am I dead? Killed in a car accident? I am concerned about my mother!

I have no memory of past events, and nobody can hear me

trying to call out so I must be dead — is this the morgue? Why else would I be here? I see someone in a bed beside me who is very still so I think she or he must be dead too and I wonder what she or he died from. I am concerned someone may come to take me away to bury me and not realise I am still alive, so I try calling out but can't get my voice to work! Dead people can't talk, so is that why my voice has gone? If I keep moving, someone may come close enough to see I am able to move, so I must be alive not dead! Or am I? Is death just being trapped in our body? No one has come over to me. *I have no voice*! I am scared and afraid wondering how will I tell someone I am alive? But am I? I should just keep thrashing my legs around, hoping eventually someone will see, so I won't be buried ... or worse, cremated! Then a thought comes into my head. OH GOD, I have four daughters! My precious girls! How are they coping? They will be devastated with my death! I wonder if they have been to identify me. Who did? Which one? I hope they all came together so the awful job was not left for only one of them. They would have needed each other so very much for that. I know they will have been a support for each other, they are good mates together. But what has happened? I wish I was able to remember it! *Please* don't let me be dead. I want to live! How long have I been dead? It must have just happened because I am still here in the morgue. There has been a terrible mistake because I am alive, so if I keep moving, I may be able to get someone's attention. I'm relieved in part, glad I am still not buried!

Chapter 12

Oh — someone is coming over to this bed. It's a nurse—HELP, HELP—no sound is coming out of my mouth! She looks at me and now she is going! She didn't even notice that I am awake — am I living in a dream? I can't call out to her, I wish she would come back, and see me alive because I can move! Oh, she *is* coming back — I think I should begin moving my legs again. When she is very close to my bed, she tells me, 'Try to stay calm, everything is okay.'

And I think, *Well, that's okay for you. What about me and my mother?* And here's a thought — What if they cremate me? I am not dead. I am alive! I am not ready to leave my girls yet! I don't know how I am going to tell anyone because I have no voice! How will I get out of this predicament? I can't even ask for a pen and paper!

Help me. I'm still alive! If I can think, I must be alive, and I can move too, or am I just in a dream? I will keep moving. Thank heavens the nurse has noticed and has begun to speak to me again, telling me to relax. She is aware I can hear her; she is nice; she tells me a doctor will come and speak to me very soon, saying they have been waiting for me to wake up.

I feel such relief and then I notice a man coming over to me. Is he here to take me away? NO! He begins talking to me and I am pleased that he also knows I am alive. I think he is a ward doctor and I like his voice; in fact, I know this voice. I feel a strange, warm comfort from his voice. I know this voice so I must know him? Where from? He begins asking me if I know what an aneurysm is. Yes, I do, but I am unable to tell him, so I nod; then he asks me if I know about cerebral aneurysms, Yes, yes, I know, but why is he talking about this to me? Has something happened to my mother?

Where is she? Has she had a cerebral bleed like her mother did? I am unable to get any words to come out of my mouth and this man with the voice I know, begins talking to me about Monique who had a cerebral aneurysm a long time ago. Why is he telling me about her and how she had a level-5 bleed when she actually had a level-3 bleed? How could he know that I know her? And why has he come to tell me about her? Maybe she is all better now? Of course, that's it! She must be in here and he is a nice man to let me know about her. I think this is how I know his voice because I would have spoken to him about Monique when it happened to her? But hasn't anyone told him that I have been in a car accident? Well, come to think of it, no one has told me either so I assume I must have killed my mother, and nobody wants to upset me, which would explain why nobody has told me. I wanted to ask this doctor with the gentle voice about my mother, but my voice wasn't coming out! After he spoke about Monique, he turned to leave the side of my bed. I remember I desperately wanted to pull him back and ask him many things and I didn't want him to go. I cried when he left, and a nurse came to wash my face.

I cried for a long time, thinking about this doctor, and although I don't have a true concept of time from then, I remember trying to fit him into where I knew his voice from.

Chapter 12

I thought about him, (seemingly) for many hours, between thoughts of my precious girls. The words this doctor had said to me kept flooding back into my head and my mind opened up to new possibilities and reality struck me. Oh *shit*, he wasn't talking about Monique — he was talking about ME! He isn't a ward doctor; he is a brain surgeon who has been inside MY head. He said he has clipped it. He said it was a level-5 bleed! Who *me*? Was this the loaded freight train in my head that I carried around for so many months? Was it me who has had a level-5 bleed? What does a brain surgeon look like? Could he be one? I have never known a brain surgeon. I have never been in that circle of people so how would I know how to recognise a brain surgeon? If I were to imagine, I think one would probably be just like this man who spoke to me with the voice I know. He seems very nice, clean and well groomed, with a gentle voice, and radiates professionalism. Is he a surgeon? He doesn't look like a man who would make up a story like that to someone like me who has been in a car accident. But have I? NO! I haven't been in a car accident, that is why nobody has told me, because it didn't happen! I am in here because it is *me* who has had the level-5 cerebral bleed! Was this the pains I carried around for so long in my head? Oh *SHIT*, what if I am unable to walk? What if I am trapped in my body like Monique? Once again, I thrash my legs about making certain they were still connected to me.

So often, over the next few weeks, I rubbed all the skin off my heels and elbows, needing gel bandages for protection. I think I thought about the nice surgeon every day, wanting him to come back so I could find out what has happened, but mostly I thought about my daughters and how I wanted to cuddle up to them. What if they have already been and gone from here and they don't know I am still ALIVE! I hoped someone would say to them — guess what? We made a mistake; your mother is alive!

Over the years, my girls have joked and called me Smother instead of Mother; have I wanted too many cuddles? I wondered if they had been to see me. I decided that next time I get a visit from those four women who are coming by a lot, I will try to *somehow* tell them to get a message to my girls. Maybe I can write it on paper for them, but now, with my voice not working, I will try to use some sign language to get a pen and paper. Who are they? They are all showing such concern so I must know them. I was unable to slot them into wherever they fitted into my life.

They know me, maybe I know their mum? So, they must also know my girls! Maybe they can get them to come and visit me? I wish my voice would work! I am so frustrated!

Oh, if only I could speak! And James, where is he? Does he know where I am? For some reason I feel the need to protect myself, but I don't know from what. It's so noisy in this place, so I want to yell out to someone to turn the volume down. I have never heard such loud noises. Why is everything so loud? And when did my hearing become so sensitive to all this noise?

Chapter 12

A woman is constantly calling out for someone. I wish I was able to tell her to just shut up! I think she should be happy she has a voice, but she is quite cranky over something. I don't know what her problem is but if I had a voice like hers, I would be over the moon! I begin to realise that she is not dead either. Maybe us live ones go on this side of the room! There are lots of smells and beeping noises! So, not only is my hearing very acute, so is my sense of smell. I am confused, tired, needing to sleep.

I think around now is when I fell back to sleep.

My thoughts were erratic, and now, looking back, I think I was a little bit mad.

Sometime later, I found out I had been in intensive care and woken after two months on life support. Amidst my confusion, I was soon trying to capture past events in an attempt to make sense of where I was, and why. I don't have much memory of events around this time yet, strangely, I do remember a lot of my thoughts.

Often wondering about the nice doctor who had spoken to me, I wished, for what seemed like an eternity, that he would come back. I thought that maybe then I could place him because I knew his voice so well. I began to think of him a lot. Was he a brain surgeon and did he save my life? Had I met him before my accident? I was confused and unable to grasp what had happened to me. I can remember having thoughts around this time but was unable to remember any events until a couple of months later when I was moved into high dependency. Once there, my memory began to return in part, very slowly, but I was still living in a constant state of confusion. I have been told about times I had climbed over the rails on the side of my bed, throwing myself onto the floor, ripping out cannulas and doing damage to myself after coming to the decision (more than once) that it was about time to get out of this hospital bed! Since I was no longer hooked up to a machine and being monitored, getting myself out of bed seemed a good idea, but resulted in many falls in the long drop from bed to floor. Me, stay in bed? Are they joking?

There were many crash landings when the pole supporting the drip also came down. I would rip the cannula out of my arm each time. I couldn't just lay there! Sadly for the staff, but good for me, my tracheal tube had been removed, which meant, not only could I climb over the sides, but also, NOW I HAD A VOICE!

So, I began speaking day and night, which is not like me at all, but I must have been overjoyed to have my voice back. I gave it a real workout, speaking a whole lot of rubbish. Was I moved into high dependency on account of now being too active for intensive care? Had I become too noisy?

James was visiting regularly and finally I realised that the four lady visitors were my daughters! I remember thinking that one of my granddaughters was my mother. She had to be, because I knew her well, but was unable to slot her into where she belonged. She was important to me, and she was female, so as far as I could work out, she must be my mother. But my granddaughter was only ten at the time!

As my condition began to improve, James organised a television for me and this brought more confusion to my damaged brain. Unable to separate fact from fantasy, I was living with a delusional state of mind. Watching a cooking show, I called to all the hospital staff to come and see my grandson from Toowoomba on his own television show. I was so proud of him but unable to understand why he would be a cook when he was a high-ranking football player who had won many awards. The nurses tried to tell me that it wasn't my grandson, it was Jamie Oliver, an English chef. This frustrated me because it was him — my grandson — surely, they realise I know my own grandson? After all, I would know better than these nurses and doctors, wouldn't I? I was still unaware of what happened to me.

I was curious that nobody seemed to be able to bring my mother in to see me — so where was she? Now that my voice was back, I asked about her and was told she was not to visit me just yet, so I assumed that something terrible had happened to her; my family were not telling me the entire story.

With my voice now returned, I was making up for lost time, and most likely I drove staff and visitors crazy, raving on about the things I had dreamt of, believing they had been actual events, until finally, to my visitors' relief, I exhausted myself, falling asleep with visitors still beside my bed (I'm told).

I was told, and believed, that my mother was in the next room and would visit me later in the day... or did I imagine this conversation? I remember calling to her over and over and there was never any response. My daughters and James have told me about some things I said to hospital staff and visitors, and most were very out of character for me, and embarrassing, to say the least. I had many dreams, one time having to be calmed down from hysteria after a bad dream about my sister who had been eaten by an elephant. This may have been due to flicking through a magazine before sleep and reading an elephant story. My brain was unable to separate fact or fantasy from fiction, making fantasy from pictures in a magazine and all without my help.

What a brain I have — it goes into auto-drive, making up some wonderful stories, some best not to mention. *Oh what an imagination I had.* I spent a lot of time in a garden with very colourful flowers, but I had a feeling they weren't real — they never moved and looked a bit plasticky. I felt they could not be picked for a pretty bouquet; what a strange thought! I was unable to process much at all in the real world.

My life was a state of mind, like a dream, yet real ... I was unaware of time and felt like I am living in someone else's space. I was still asking about the nice doctor I had met some time back. Had I dreamt him up also? Sometime later, my girls and James told me about their meeting with the 'nice doctor' and I was relieved to know I hadn't also dreamt him up. I was so pleased to be told he was real and that he was my surgeon. I since learnt that the comfort I felt from his voice must have been from hearing him while I had been in a coma. Did my subconscious mind save it and store it somehow? Is this the difference between memory and recall? I couldn't have remembered him because I had never met him, so it must be recall from just hearing him.

James and my girls told me of their first meeting with him three months prior when I had been bought to hospital by ambulance after I had collapsed from a seizure similar to that of a grand mal. At the hospital, my family were met by two neuro interns who explained to them that I had had a large cerebral aneurysm, and it was about to burst open. This would more than likely kill me if it ruptured inside my head, but I may live if lucky. They were also told that if I survived, I may have little or no control over my body and its functioning. In other words, I would be a vegetable, like my neighbour Monique.

Later, James told me about the night when all efforts were made for a neurosurgeon to undertake life-saving surgery, but none were available on short notice. Beside this, it was late in the afternoon and such surgery required a well-rested team. The only alternative was to send me to another hospital for the surgery. Plans were made to send me by helicopter to another hospital out west. I am told that James was with me while waiting for clearance for the helicopter when the cerebral aneurysm swelled in my head and was about to burst, causing another seizure as had happened a few hours earlier when I was taken to the hospital. James became sick and began to vomit. After the convulsions subsided, my girls were told that I was possibly dying and were sent in to say goodbye to me. They were told I would still be sent by the hospital helicopter to a hospital out west, but that there was no guarantee I would survive the trip as I was already now damaged from the swelling aneurism which could break open at any time and cause a major haemorrhage. My family gave consent for this and were told where I would be taken by helicopter. Finally, I was visited by a priest before clearance and my family all set out for the other hospital, a long drive away.

On their arrival, they were told that I'd never arrived, which caused great concern for them because after many phone calls between hospitals it was discovered that a senior neurosurgeon — Dr Chandler — had been located at the hospital where I was to stay and he would treat me; he would not allow a trip in the helicopter, saying that it was far too risky. I am told he kept me alive by placing me in an induced coma and had slowed my pulse to very low to ease pressure of my blood flow. My family returned to the hospital but were not appraised by him, instead it came from the two neuro-interns whom they had seen earlier that night. They told my family that they were unaware if I could hear while in a coma, but advised them to talk to me, saying it may make a difference and hopefully if I was still alive the following day, then Dr Chandler would operate. Again, it was stressed that there was no guarantee that I would live through the night, and if I did, no guarantee I would survive such dangerous surgery, and no knowledge of my level of body functioning after surgery.

My girls were concerned that I may end up living in a useless body, so were very afraid to make the wrong decision, knowing that if I survived the night and had to have surgery the next day, I may not survive the ordeal. I had said many times over the years to not ever let me live like Monique, saying if that ever happened to me, just let me die. I was far too active to be living like the living dead, and 'better off dead', I had often said. It was James who talked them around to agreeing on the surgery for me, I am told he said I was 'strong and deserved a fighting chance. If *anyone* can survive this your mother can, she is a strong woman and deserves this chance!'

For many years I had felt like a default to James, feeling we were never connected, and there was always something ugly hovering in our relationship, yet maybe he knew me better that I gave him credit for, knowing I would fight to survive.

If I lived through the night until morning, I would get the lifesaving surgery. James had earlier phoned Leigh in Toowoomba and organised a flight for her to come to Sydney to be here with her sisters, in case I didn't survive. She arrived that night soon after my family had first met Dr Chandler — the man with the lovely gentle voice. Fate must have planned for me to be in the right place at this time in my life because

I consider myself the luckiest person on earth to have been operated on by this man.

The following morning ... Sunday, on my entry into the operating theatre, the aneurysm broke open. Before surgery, Dr Chandler explained the procedure to my family, telling them that my chance of survival was only six percent. James was right in telling my girls that if anyone could survive this, then I could, and I did, surviving the eleven-hour surgery.

This was followed over the next few months by further brain surgery arising from other issues. Then came the strokes caused by further operations on my brain. Those strokes shut down the left side of my body. After a little shy of three months in a coma, I was out of intensive care and moved to high dependency where I have memories from a mostly conscious state and maybe a few from my life through dreaming. To this day, I'm still not sure which was a dream, and which was an actual event. In high dependency I am told I had caused great concern for staff and medical teams with my independent efforts, throwing myself out of bed on many occasions and trying to do the impossible.

The bleed had occurred from a ruptured cerebral aneurysm in the subarachnoid space, which is between the middle and inner layer of the brain and full of delicate web-like tissue cushioned by cerebrospinal fluid and in the temporal lobe, hence my memory loss that was to follow. Dr Chandler had explained to them before surgery that I would most likely have ongoing neurological deficits and loss of function in my body, and the possibility of a stroke that could follow such surgery was high. He was right! Bleeding into the brain will usually cause death as it had done to my grandmother.

The next day, after many long hours of intense surgery, Dr Chandler had clipped the artery where the bleed had occurred and told my family again of a possible stroke after such surgery. Some weeks after this, the strokes came and shut down the left side of my body. I stayed in high dependency, sleeping for most of the day and unable to separate dreams from reality — my life became a work in progress!

The aneurism that had burst that night was a level-5 bleed — very dangerous — and despite my family being told I would possibly be dead by the morning, I survived and am still here! With all the events that have come into play since then, I am very grateful.

Chapter 13

With the confusion of my parallel life, I am in awe of how I am able to recall my thoughts from that time; some so strange it's best not to talk (or write) about. Yet I am unable to remember actual happenings. I am able to remember absurd dreams that often woke me. One dream in particular, which has stayed firm in my memory, is my being somewhere with very large gates, not the pearly gates, but more like the gates of Buckingham Palace, black and topped with gold. I got close to them, holding onto them; I remember how cold they felt to my touch. Beyond the gates I saw a long dark hallway which seemed to have light coming out of open doors along the way. I saw James' father walking up the hallway towards me. I was so pleased to see him again but shocked to see my own father close behind. When they got closer to me, I tried to push the gates open. I wanted to embrace my father, but James' father raised his hand indicating to stop, telling me to turn and go back. I felt hurt when he didn't seem to want me to go inside, and I remember thinking, how is this happening?

Chapter 13

What are they doing here? How did they get here? They are both dead! Where am I? What are all the lights?

I had a feeling of gladness, pleased that my father and James' father had finally met as I knew they'd get along well together. I wondered, *Was I stuck in a time warp?* It was so quiet there, so peaceful ... and though my father was pleased to see me, he told me, 'You should not be here, so go away.' I wondered why ... *Was it just because James' father had also told me to turn and go? What is wrong with them? How come they don't want me here?* Then, without feeling anything or knowing how it happened, I was somewhere way above the coastline, up in the sky and looking down on the Nuns' Pool where my mother and I had spent so many days together years ago with my children. Then, somehow, I was suddenly beside a lake somewhere else, skimming stones with David, a friend of Marie's. He was asking me, 'Please tell Marie I am sorry... please say sorry to Marie for me.'

I told him I could not get involved. 'Whatever has happened between the two of you, it is up to you to tell her sorry — not me. Don't involve me!'

David was paying board while living in a spare room at Marie's place. I thought he might have spilt something on the carpet, or may not have mown the lawns, or maybe he spoke rudely to her. He told me he couldn't face her. I said, 'Oh my god David, what have you done that is so bad that you can't face her?'

He didn't want to tell me, but eventually said, 'Marie will

know by now and I am very sorry for it.' Again, he begged me to tell Marie how sorry he was. Soon after this conversation with him, I was beside the Nuns' Pool again, where I had many picnics with my mother and swam with my girls when they were little. I seemed to be in places very quickly, but I still don't know how I got to each place, nor do I know how I soon became stuck in a hole, buried up to my neck in sand, gasping to get breath into me.

David appeared from somewhere and began dragging the sand away to ease the pressure around my chest, enabling me to breathe and to escape. How did this happen? I don't remember falling into any hole! I have strong memories of David frantically digging, trying to get me out. I was feeling heavy and unable to get enough air into my lungs. There was great relief when he was able to get the sand away — I could breathe, and I was soon out. I began running over the sand hills searching for my mother, worried I had come too far, knowing deep down my mother wouldn't be all this way from the Nuns' Pool. Then, somehow, I was back up in the sky so high, looking down on the coastline. I enjoyed the view but, how did I suddenly get to be so high up? I could see the coastline and the deep valley-type cracks in the ground, some with huge water-filled holes with massive boulders in them. I became frightened, remembering a time I had been trapped down one of these holes and unable to climb out. I can still feel the terror of being trapped in a hole, afraid they would soon be filling with water. Did something like this really happen to me at some time because I can picture every rock, every large pool and the depth of the water, the size of the rocks and the colour of the water, and I can still feel the fear I had from it. Soon, up in the air again, I was able to see so many little islands with the surf pounding on rocks and the long coastline, stretching for many miles.

Months later, on a day when Marie was looking after me, I remembered seeing David somewhere, but wasn't sure when or where. So, I asked Marie why I hadn't seen him, vaguely telling her that the last time I saw him was at the beach, before I had been in hospital. Once I said that though, I felt like I was lying because I knew he wasn't really a beach person. I vividly remembered skimming stones with him and the hole he got me out of. I remembered our conversation and his asking me to say sorry to Marie, but I was unable to put this conversation into a time slot, nor form the words properly, so I asked Marie, 'Where is David? Why haven't I seen him? Has he moved out?'

After telling Marie I had seen David not long ago, she told me I couldn't have seen him because I had been in hospital for the past few months. But I *had* seen David and I told her that he had said he was sorry. Marie began crying, telling me that when I was in hospital, David had taken his own life. Was this the reason he was unable to face her, the reason he almost begged me to tell her he was sorry? Did I experience some kind of divine visitation? Where was I when he spoke to me? Where was I when we were skimming stones, and when I was buried up to my neck and he dug me out?

At the time, I was home most days, and I didn't know which day of the week it was until I snuck out to the corner shop to read the day and date on the front of the newspaper. I was unable remember what I did yesterday, so I wondered how I could remember dreams and even some thoughts from my time in hospital.

Chapter 14

I find memory so amazing because another thing I remember (or recall?) is that while in hospital, I was visited every day by a little girl who sat in the chair beside my bed. I am not sure if it was when I was in high dependency or earlier in intensive care. Although I had no concept of time, I remember her vividly. I had never seen her before this time, so I didn't know who she was, thinking the children's ward must be close for her to visit so often. Sitting in the big armchair beside my bed, which made her appear so small, her legs didn't reach the floor — she would smile at me, so I would say hello to her.

One day, I told her how clever I thought she was to be able to find me every day and I asked her a few things, but there was never an answer — she never spoke to me, she'd just give me a beautiful smile. I wondered why she was in hospital because she didn't look very sick to me, and I told her to be careful, because she was a bit young to be wandering around the hospital on her own and could get lost. Many times, I asked her name to no avail, so instead I asked for her mummy's name. 'Do I know your mummy and is that how you know me?' Still no response and yet the daily visits continued. I asked her if the children's ward was too noisy for her and was that why she came to sit beside me each day?

Another day, a nurse came into my room and pointed to all the pretty pictures on the wall that the little girl must have drawn when no one was watching. The nurse made a hand gesture, saying, 'Oh my god, how are you going to get through all of this?' She also said she had never seen anything quite like it, nor had she ever seen so much. This poor little girl who visited me daily was now getting the blame for the many lovely drawings all over the wall. I wondered how she drew them, being too little to reach up the walls. The drawings were also more like what an adult would draw, so I thought how clever she was, and assumed she must have dragged a chair over to stand on. I decided to defend her, but the nurse seemed to become snappy about it, so I told her not to blame the little girl and covered for her by remarking that she always simply sat there without speaking and couldn't reach that height anyway, which was met with a 'Tut tut'.

The next time the little girl visited, I told her that I'd help her clean them all off, and for her not to worry.

I was having many visitors but not sure who they were. Most people coming to my bed were familiar, but I was unable to place any of them. I was so tired, needing sleep, so I was often falling asleep when I had visitors. Most mornings (against my wishes) I was propped in a chair to be taken out

Chapter 14

for the day (I thought), but in actual fact, was taken to rehab where I was being taught how to walk and balance myself. I was also being taught how to get up and down stairs. I learnt colours, shapes, and names of things in picture books. While there I met many people and had conversations about events. I was asked a lot about my life and my family. Sometimes I was given a box with coloured blocks of different shapes. Sometimes I was given pencils and pretty picture books to do some colouring but was told which colour to use. I wished they would just let me choose my own colours, but I enjoyed doing it just the same.

One person I met in rehab was an older man who kept forgetting his birth date and always gave the wrong answer when asked. He seemed to become so disappointed in himself and I didn't like to see him upset so I told him my date, telling him to simply use mine and that no one would know. This fell apart when a lady who worked there told me she knew the man was lying about the year at least because he was a good thirty years older than the year I was born.

When taken back to my room, I'd drift into zombie mode, needing to sleep from exhaustion, but someone always wanted to ask me all about my day in rehab. Days out for me were hard and I was so tired. I became frustrated when most people couldn't understand what I was saying. This was because my tongue now weighed a ton, which made speaking very difficult. I could tell my little girl visitor about my days in rehab because at least she knew what I was saying, however, no one else seemed to understand me. When dinner time came, I was fed by a nurse.

One day, I had a visitor whom I was more than happy to welcome. *Oh my goodness!* I was over the moon with excitement as it was Kylie Minogue! I remember thinking, this is the *best* thing that has happened for me in such a long time (oh yes!) — my favourite entertainer. I couldn't believe it when she told me she was getting married and that she'd like me to come to her wedding. Can you believe it? I was so happy because she was and is my *favourite* person from television and music. I always went to her concerts, telling my friends on many occasions: 'We all dream for something very special — I want to meet Kylie one day! I just love her, and this is going on my bucket list. When it happens, I can tell her how much I love her.' I had often told my girls that one day (somehow), I would meet Kylie, and I suspect that my daughters were a little jealous of my admiration for her. So, on this day, I was beside myself with excitement when she visited me to ask me to her wedding. She said I should wear my new gold high heels, the ones I had bought a couple of months back. I was amazed that she knew about my new shoes — how did she know? We must have a connection, I decided. I didn't know anyone who could have told her because I didn't think she knew any of my friends, yet it must have been them who organised this lovely surprise for me; the same friend who told her about my new gold high heels. I couldn't wait to tell my family, and I told anyone and everyone who came to visit

Chapter 14

about my visit from Kylie Minogue. Yes, yes, she had come to visit *me*! Wow, she even asked me to her wedding! Oh yes, I was so excited! Then I thought about this, the most exciting event in my life for ages. I even told the rehab doctor, the one who always wanted to know who the prime minister was or what year it was. Sadly, my family told me I had dreamt it all up. Why would they say such a thing? I wasn't making it up — I *saw* her, *spoke* to her! I couldn't understand why they would tell me it wasn't true! Why on earth would they say something like that, knowing it would hurt me? I felt devastated and cried in disappointment.

Soon after this event in my life, I was given more surgery to install a ventriculoperitoneal (VP) shunt in my head to drain away cerebrospinal fluid that had accumulated, causing pressure on my brain. Apparently, the pressure was responsible for my imaginary visit from Kylie. Again, so disappointing, though I am pleased to have met her in my own funny kind of way.

I was living in a confused state of mind with very little grasp on reality and this could be also the reason I had been visited by the little blonde girl — another divine visitation? The 'drawings' on the wall were actually my get-well cards, sent to me from so many people. It seemed I had become quite mad before the shunt had been installed in my head.

After the surgery to install the drainage tubes in my head, the left side of my body lost its functioning, and it was noted I had suffered another stroke. My family was informed that

I would have residual physical deficit and unreliable memory. (Now, after nine years working on my body — and my mind — I can slowly respond to most requests and can now walk unaided, alone, carefully and slowly, still with limitations, and sometimes, difficulties. With prompting, I am able to use my left side on most occasions, which improves with each passing month. I think of Dr Chandler with much appreciation, grateful to the powers that brought him into my life.)

One day in hospital, one of my girls told me that Dudley sent his love and was missing me. Oh yes, I have a beautiful dog! I began to miss him and worry that he may be wondering where on earth I was. I became concerned, curious, wondering who was looking after him; walking him; throwing a ball in the park with him; feeding him. I knew he would be missing me so I asked James if Dudley could come to the hospital to visit.

We all knew Dudley was a dog, but Dudley was very much unaware of that fact, even after he'd been told so many times. For a dog who understood most words of the English language, I still don't think he was ever aware that he was different to us. He doesn't go to work, sleeps on a mattress on the floor, eats from a bowl on the floor, but I still think that he thinks he is one of us — poor Duddles! The next day I was taken by wheelchair to the outside kiosk for a visit from Dudley. I was close to crying with excitement, keen to let him know I was still around. On arrival at the outside kiosk, when he saw me he became very anxious and although sitting, he was marking time with his front legs, whimpering in anticipation. I knew he wanted to run over and jump up on me, but he was aware I was not well enough and when James tried to bring him closer to me, he wouldn't come near me. Maybe because I was now smelling like a hospital and not Chanel No 5 as I had done in the past. Soon, he came near me, and I was able to pat and talk to him. I was glad he now knew I hadn't deserted him. I hoped his sixth sense would tell him I would be home soon, as if I kept improving, I'd be allowed a weekend trial run at home and see how we all coped.

After four months in hospital, I was allowed home. Firstly though, a few safety measures needed to be met.

An occupational therapist came to the house to compile a list of things needing to be changed in order to make the house safe for me. This entailed mounting rails on most of the walls to assist my walks to various rooms. All of the mats had to be taken up and an A-frame installed in the toilet to assist my balance. All bulky items had to be removed to avoid bumping into anything, so all my large plants were now moved outside. The hot water was to be lowered in temperature to save me being scalded. A safety shut-off switch in the electrical box was installed to avoid electrical accidents. Many other adjustments were to be made in order to make our house a safe place for me.

Sadly, I don't have a memory of this weekend at home except for the memory of being unable to master the staircase and having to crawl up the sixteen stairs to my bedroom. In hindsight though, this memory may have come from two weeks later, when I *was* finally allowed home. I would not let any of my family assist me on my journey up the stairs and went up on my hands and knees, crawling and crying with exhaustion, but determined to reach the top, on my own! This must have been frustrating for my family to watch, especially when they wanted to help, but I would not allow that. The sixteen stairs that I would run up in the past had now become one of my biggest challenges. My girls and James prepared our home as required, and once discharged, my new life was about to begin.

My daughters and James were all very supportive, probably not entirely realising the mammoth job they were now faced with. Between them all, a roster was created for each person's turn of duty; each of them having their day with me. I was given a note pad and biro in order to write down anything I was in need of before I had forgotten what it was. I was unable to do anything on my own and needed daily assistance to shower, feed, toilet and dress myself. I couldn't clean my teeth or do anything that required two hands. I'd miss my mouth when I tried to put food in, and the food went over my shoulder or up my nostril ... I was not aware how far my arms could reach and I couldn't get them to move when I wanted them to. My left arm seemed to have a mind of its own. I recall the many times I had to push it down from across the front of me, but it would only creep back across my chest with

Chapter 14

my hand all curled up. I couldn't place anything down evenly with my right hand, so everything I put down ended up on the floor or falling over. When I picked up a fallen object, I'd drop it again and would become frustrated. Unable to process fast enough to hold a conversation, I needed extra time to answer people, then forgot what I wanted to say.

If I thought my rehab in hospital was hard and tiring, it was nothing compared to the battle I was now facing. The fight of my life was about to begin. Over the following weeks, month, and years, I learned the true meaning of words such as — frustration, patience, tired, pain, prayer and ZOMBIE!

In the past, I had taken many things for granted — now, each day I am placed in front of the television for comfort. I watch whatever is on, now unable to process how to work the remote, which I threw across the room with frustration more than once! I was getting a constant stream of visitors and always fell asleep on their visits! They brought dinner and cakes, offering to help in any way. Do some washing? Vacuum? Hose the garden maybe? Take me for a walk? All meaning well, but I was slipping back into a zombie state, falling asleep, unable to stay awake. Some would toilet me, giving my family some much-needed help. Embarrassing for me!

Dudley kept watch on anyone who came near me and was at my side, positioning himself between me and whoever was assisting me, not letting me even get to another room without being at my side. I think he was worried I may leave him again.

One day, a friend came to give me a leg and foot massage, which was the most painful touch I'd ever felt, feeling like she was rubbing me with sandpaper and taking my skin off. No chance of relaxing through that. I never told her though and she will only know if she reads this. My body had become so sensitive to all touch, especially my left side. Most touch hurts me, and yet some I couldn't feel. My showers each morning are no longer looked forward to like I did before. Now I fear showering! Showers bring pain and discomfort, each drop of water falling on me feeling like a splinter of glass slicing into my skin. So, during this time I cry in pain. After my showers, James dries me, and the towel being rubbed on me feels like sandpaper ripping my skin off. I have torn the rotator cuff in my left shoulder and was told this tear may have been from throwing myself out of the hospital bed on more than one occasion. My poor girls and James need to keep watch on me. Maria has me at her place one or two days a week while she runs her business from home and I don't say anything, but I would rather be in my own home because on the days at her place I am missing Dudley; knowing he would be missing me, afraid I may have gone for an extended time again. I didn't say this to anyone, thinking that no one would have understood.

James had recently started a new job in a hotel, and it was hard for him to get time off. He sometimes had to sleep over after a late lockup, and on those nights, I'd sleep at his sister's place where his mother now lived. She looked after me the following day when James was at work. On some nights when

Chapter 14

I wanted to stay home with Dudley, another of James' sisters would come over to stay the night with me in my home. His family and mother, in particular, were all very good to me. When my girls needed to be at work, or were unable to have me, Thursday became my regular day to be cared for by James' mother. Some other days, after James showered, dressed and fed me, he'd take me to his mother's place so he could go to work. Many times, I thought that having to do so much for me was hard for James, who had never been a father, so had never needed to do anything in such a capacity before. One night a week, when James had a late lock up and had to sleep over at work, Joanne had her turn to stay with me.

Raelene had changes made to her roster and was now able to care for me some days, so I was very lucky to have such help. I tried to regain my life, but my physical balance was not good, and I had many falls, which was a constant reminder that nothing was the same anymore. I became angry with God, wondering why He would allow such a thing to happen to me. I had such a battle getting my body to work properly again. When I complained about God to Joanne, I am proud of her explanation, telling me that I was not experiencing punishment from God for anything. Instead, God saved me from certain death and incapacities and now I must keep improving. She is certainly a born teacher. My girls became my heart healers with the care that they were keen and able to give me. I have been told many times how lucky I am to have the daughters that every mother dreams to have.

These days, I am unable to keep up with a conversation, finding it impossible (just yet) to process like I could before all this happened to me. I remind myself of Joanne's explanation, which helps me to get on with things, even though at times I felt my life had lost all of its colour ...

Chapter 15

While I had been in hospital, my sister visited our mother on her way home from work. One night, she found Mum on the bathroom floor, bleeding from a gash to her head and with a possible broken hip. Paramedics were called and she was taken to hospital where she was admitted, awaiting surgery. Her left hip was fractured just as the right hip had been months before. After surgery to repair her hip and a few days in hospital, the time came for her to be discharged. This had all happened while I was in a coma, when there was no one to care for her, so my sister had no choice but to place her into an aged care facility (which Mum would have hated, had she been aware). A month after her hip surgery, my sister was able to get Mum placed in a home close to both of our homes. This aged care facility was built on the paddock behind the shack where my friend Jenny from school had lived, and where the horse she was minding was kept during the days when we all galloped around the shire on horseback.

While in care, Mum had been sick with concern wondering

what had happened to me. When she was told, and as soon as she possibly could, she began phoning the hospital every hour. Worn thin, soon they told Mum that she was tying up the lines with her constant phone calls every hour. These were the calls that I would normally (abnormally) receive on a daily basis. I was told she was fretting for me, begging to come and visit while I was in intensive care. My family had been advised by the medical team that because of the pressure she had placed on me before all this happened, she was not to visit just yet. Also, taking her age into consideration, for her to see me with tubes coming out of my head, throat, nose and linked to beeping machines, might be too much for her to accept so it was decided to wait until I looked a bit better.

A few months later, she was able to visit. I have a memory of my sister bringing her to visit, but it is only a flash with no real detail; however, I remember she wore a mauve dress that I had bought for her about a year before.

Now at home, I am trying to do too much, so I am regularly falling over, usually hurting myself and am often taken to the local outpatients for stitches on my head where I have gashed it open on many occasions. One time I knocked myself unconscious after falling onto our pot belly heater. At hospital, I was told by the emergency doctor that I was lucky I didn't kill myself and I should appreciate my second chance of life and stop making things hard for my family.

Oh my god! He has *no* idea how hard my life had become. I wanted to hit the doctor for saying this to me, as I'd been trying to get normality back. James had told me on many occasions how hard it was for him and the girls, which made me want to do more without asking them as I didn't want to be a bother for them like Mum had become for me at times.

I wanted to remain in my own home throughout the recovery, but after a few months at home, sadly my girls were unable to be with me every day, so it was then time for James to pay for home help, which was Claire — a friend and a wonderful help. She took Dudley and me for walks and would do anything in the home that needed to be done. Claire cooked, washed, gardened, and every second day she took me to visit my mother in the nursing home. After ten months when Claire's husband became sick and was rushed to hospital, she had to care for him.

James said we needed another minder, but I begged him to trust me to stay home alone. I hadn't been stitched from a fall for a few months (they didn't know about some of the falls!). I hadn't told my family about my walks alone in the afternoons when I would take Dudley because he would drop his lead in front of me. None of my family were aware of my outings, nor how I was unable to stay within the two-and-a-half-metre width of pedestrian crossings, often going outside the boundary stripes looking like a drunk person because I was over-correcting my steps to stay within the width. Sometimes, someone I knew would drive me home and I would ask them to keep it secret and not tell James. But unbeknown to me, some people we knew passed by, so it wasn't long before my family were told about my outings.

I was made to promise I wouldn't leave the house alone again. *Are you kidding?* I thought to myself, *They would have to bolt me down to keep me from going out.*

One day, I became stuck in the middle of a busy road. I was terrified. Luckily, Raelene had put my phone on a lanyard to wear around my neck for quick and easy access, so I was able to phone Marie to come and get me while I hung onto the pole in the middle of the road, crying while cars sped by, some tooting the horn. When Marie arrived, she told me I looked like a frightened lost girl just hanging on; well, I was. I was soon told that if I wanted to stay home alone, I would need to *promise* to stay in the house where I would be safe. Is it true that promises are made to be broken? Because not even that demand stopped me. I went for many walks, not alone because Dudley was with me. Other days I would catch a taxi to visit my mother, but soon, I became afraid of the drivers. Especially one in particular who looked like a man on the television, now charged with the murder of a backpacker in the Northern Territory. At the time, this had dominated the news and somewhere in my unbalanced thought process, I thought the taxi driver was planning to take me away and meet this man from the television, whereby they both would then kill me. Why else was it always the same driver who came to pick me up? This fear overwhelmed me many times. Sometimes on the way home from visiting Mum, I'd be in fear of the driver,

Chapter 15

and I'd tell him to pull over so I could get out, afraid, but not knowing why. Now I realise it was anxiety, knowing I was not strong enough to defend myself if needed. Sometimes I was miles away from any train station or bus stop and had to walk for a long, long way. Once or twice, I wet myself (and the other) before reaching the station. I had many embarrassing outings that I wish I could forget, but then, I am glad to recall how hard everything was because it gives me a certain appreciation. I was a work in progress — my recovery has been such a journey.

Looking back to those days, I can see why James was concerned that I wasn't a well person. When home, I would sometimes ring James to tell him that someone had been following me with the intent of killing me. One time I thought the visitors over the road were people coming to kidnap me, and that they were just hiding in the house across the road waiting for the right time to get me. So, it came as no surprise when an appointment was made for me to talk to a psychiatrist, who told me that my brain had been through a lot of shock and trauma and that I'd placed such huge expectations on myself, saying also that I should be proud of my achievements so far.

After almost eighteen months at home, my visits to the hospital for stitches are not so frequent, but my black eyes from trip-ups and slips are a common sight; at times my body became so tired that it was hard to function on any level. I'd often go into zombie mode with every day feeling like ground-hog day.

I shared secrets with Dudley on the nights before my brain haemorrhage when I drank alone. Now, he was hearing about my frustrations of my body no longer working like it should. I had always been a very active person, going to a gym three or four times weekly, and now (apart from my sneaking out of the house) the extent of my physical activities is my supported walks to the bathroom for a bladder or a bowel movement. I often cried with frustration when I tried to hang some washing on the line, dropping pegs and whatever it was that was meant to go onto the line, then falling over when I attempted to pick them up, not once or twice, but over and over, many times. I was not giving in!

Time dragged, I was always so tired, and I looked forward to the end of each day so that I could go to bed. I would cry with frustration. Although I was frustrated, James told me I shouldn't be angry or fed up, and sick of trying to do things every day with everything now a struggle. James wasn't fully aware of my struggles and how hard everything had become for me. In fact, nobody knew how hard *everything* was for me to do because I never complained, mainly because I didn't want to be told how negative I had become. It made me feel worse when told I was negative and getting bitter, so I was soon careful not to ask anyone for help with anything. Sadly, with all the good he has, I felt James was yet to know the difference between disappointment in oneself and frustration, which he considered to be bitterness and being negative.

When I was alone, I cried a lot. I had knitted for my

grandchildren and others, so I tried to knit, but dropped stitches — sometimes the complete row of stitches slipped off the needle and I'd lose all that I had painstakingly achieved, so I'd cry. I was also unable to use my sewing machine on account of losing my fine motor skills, leaving me unable to thread the machine. Even if I could get someone to thread it for me, I still was unable to use it because I couldn't guide the material under the needle and use the foot pedal at the same time, so again I became a crying mess.

Because of this, I found a place in my head to store my pain and frustrations, calling it my 'deadwood pile', saying it was for dealing with later. When I eventually told James about this, he again told me how bitter I am because I never had a deadwood pile before. My response was that I'd never had a brain bleed before and that I was just trying to cope the best way I could.

My daughters and I began to call my left hand 'Thing' like the hand in The Adams family that was kept on a bench alone because it seemed to have a mind of its own, doing its own thing, so , after some odd movements from my left hand it was now decided to be called "thing".

I was pleased one day when James said we needed to move into the hotel that he was managing so we could at last have our house renovated. I had been having reflective thoughts about my life but now I was looking forward to having our house renovated. James and I borrowed the money and moved out to make the renovation easier for the workmen, who were arriving early each day to pull down walls. It was best for us all to be out of the way and best for me not to see what was happening in my home. I decided to not tell my mother of our move into the hotel, knowing she would be very unsettled to know I was so far from her. We emptied our house by putting our furniture into the garage before moving into the hotel in the eastern suburbs.

Life took a turn (for the better) for me when I became friends with Janice, the wife of a mate of James, whom I had met at a function three weeks before my bleed. I instantly liked her and since we were now living such a long way from James' mother, I was no longer going to her for care. Janice came over to the hotel each Thursday and we would walk together. Janice and I walked all over the eastern suburbs, and I was soon able to get the train over to visit my mother, who still thought she was in a hospital. I found it best to let my mother go on thinking this way, especially since I had promised her on many occasions that I would never put her into a nursing home. Sadly, she needed full-time care and was unable to live alone safely. I was in no way able to assist her to do anything. Soon though, we needed to find new accommodation for her when the nursing home was to be pulled down and rebuilt. I was pleased that we were able to relocate Mum into the nursing home where I had been working when I started getting my headaches. I knew from working there that it was a good facility with constant staff training and updated courses in aged care, covering all areas of the aging process. Mum had stayed there a year before for respite care when advised by my boss that I should find some relief from her while I had head pain, so my work friends already knew her. She hated it back then, but she had been very demanding on me at the time. She wouldn't allow anyone to shower her, saying: 'Oh no, my daughter works here so she will shower me!' I was pleased that she didn't remember, and I didn't remind her.

My mother took around six weeks to start settling into her new surroundings, but sadly, a year later she was showing signs of dementia with the added constant urinary tract infections and slow bowel movements, causing her to become quite toxic and confused. This was coupled with antibiotic resistance, which was possibly due to overloading her system for many years with antibiotic treatment. She developed a Methicillin-resistant Staphylococcus aureus (MRSA) infection, which was active in her left eye, and not surprisingly, it seemed to have taken up residency, and was not moving. Poor Mum now looked like a little frail lost person, so I was pleased that my move into the hotel was not known by her. While living at the hotel, I had acupuncture on my frozen shoulder which gave me a great deal of pain and restricted all arm movements. Thankfully, it was slowly repairing.

Because of the pain in my body, cognitive limitations, and not much balance, I was still unable to dress myself, so James was still my primary care person and I feared that it may drive him away from me, since our talk of marriage, planned some months before, was now never mentioned. I went to bed very early those days getting much-needed sleep after my hours of walking around with Janice or Dudley. Walking and writing were all I could do without asking for help, though it placed me in zombie mode from tiredness. While living in the hotel, I met many interesting people in the bar as well as in the streets when out walking. Sadly, James and I were unable to agree on anything for our house renovations, he not liking anything I suggested, so to prevent disappointment, I stopped suggesting, but I was beginning to feel far away from him again.

Mum's dementia increased in her aging years. Although visited often by Ruby, Anne and Jenny, she sometimes slept throughout the entire visit, most days unable to be awake long enough to eat her favourite ice cream that Ruby usually bought for her. Sadly, she'd drop the ice cream in her lap. We were all aware that she had become like a small child, but fortunately, she herself was unaware of her condition. I was upset to see my beautiful mother now in her aging body; this once-effervescent woman, now so sleepy on most days. Some days it was hard to leave her because she would cling to me and cry: *'Please* don't leave me!' So, I would sit with her for a further few hours until she became sleepy. When I'd tell her I was going to the cake shop to buy her a chocolate éclair (her favourite) she again would grab my arm and plead with me not to leave, reminding me of the days when my daughters were first taken to school, and they'd hang onto my legs to keep me from leaving them. I remember that awful aching in my chest and how I had to peel them off me, just as I needed to do with my mother on these days. The other thing that saddened me was the fact I was unable to embrace her, and I wondered if I'd ever let go of pain carried from so long ago. I know I had forgiven her, yet I was still not able to embrace her. I gradually learned that to forgive is not a complete feeling because I have forgiven people in my life but have not forgotten the hurt from them.

I realised my mother may be taken from this life on earth soon, yet I still couldn't cuddle her. A kiss hello and goodbye was the best I could do, and I felt that our life had become a role reversal. I remembered the aching when I only got a kiss goodnight if all jobs were done to her satisfaction. When I visited her in the nursing home, she usually gave me orders; outside of her demented state of mind, this was the mother I had when I was a little girl — the bossy mum who handed out kisses only when jobs were done to her satisfaction, yet later, she loved and embraced her grandchildren ... unconditionally!

In my last few days at the hotel, I decided to walk with Dudley past the house where Mum was raised by an auntie who taught my mother the only 'love language' she knew. I then walked around to the public school, and the high school she had attended. I watched the kids playing in the playground and in my mind's eye I imagined how my mother would have looked so many years ago. Then I walked to where she and my father were married. While so deep in thought again, in my mind's eye I was able to see them standing in the doorway with my mother a radiant, beautiful bride. The photograph of this day had been shown to me so many times that I could almost hear church bells ringing. Walking around the streets where my mother grew up, I became full of curious thoughts, and I wondered why I was doing this. Was I trying to purge disappointments in my attempt to get past childhood hurt?

Passing the house where she had grown up, I remember the many times my mother told me how she had no love from her mother, who was too busy to care for her and who spent nights in the city, dancing in the bars or playing the pianos. My mother had been able to put so much hurt away, so why couldn't I? I knew I needed to get past many things so I could embrace my mother, realising that she now needed to feel love as I had needed her love when I was little. I knew that two wrongs didn't make things right. I didn't want my emotions to induce the wrong feelings, nor did I want to be damaged by them, or to be holding onto insoluble hurt from childhood years. My mother was able to forgive her mother and never carried anger from feeling neglected, so I told myself to get out of my own way, to grow up and get over it!

Next time I visited my mother I intended to cuddle her and tell her I loved her, to which she would say: 'Oh yes, I know you do! Now when can I move in and live with you?' I would lie again by saying: 'We will get you packed up very soon and you can come and live with me.' Mum was pleased that I finally saw how I needed her to care for me since my brain haemorrhage and she wanted to look after me, which I think was a little late, but I must let go of all that. I continued with this charade about her moving in with me to keep her in a happy frame of mind.

I met many new friends in the nine months living in the hotel, but we were now looking forward to returning home. Feeling so much stronger since our stay in the hotel, I saw how this was a huge turning point in my recovery. I was ready to get back, and looking forward to enjoying time with my shire friends. I had also decided to attend church when back home, telling myself if my father was watching down on me, he would just have to accept that I needed to thank the universe for my survival and for bringing Dr Chandler into my life. Or maybe I have a guardian angel?

When we were back home, I attempted swimming in our newly painted pool. Dudley, (the most loved dog in the universe) was more pleased than anyone. My memory was now much sharper and my balance a little better, so my walks in the park were not just a time of falling or losing my phone or my keys to get back into my house, proving to provide gentle exercise.

A few years afterwards, my body mishaps were happening much less. I had improved enough to be no longer wetting myself as often or having accidents with my bowels. I was much stronger in body and mind, and I felt it was time for me to return to my gym classes to do some yoga, especially that I'm now an experienced and confident public transport user. Soon, I was looking forward to my yoga class each Tuesday morning after which I visited Mum. I still tried to embrace her and hope the hurt I have carried from feeling unloved and rejected by her will remain in the past where it belongs. Since my brain haemorrhage, I have promised myself to no longer live in an emotional vacuum — it is time for me to be emotionally clever, to do what is the right thing instead of carrying destructive emotional pain.

I felt a change within myself. I felt stronger, although it still seemed as though my wedding to James was never going to happen, because he never mentioned it. I had bought my dress when one of his sisters took me to the shops and it hung in my wardrobe, looking like it would stay there, unused. I didn't think I should bring up the topic of a wedding as I didn't want to handle any hurt the conversation would bring, as it had in the past. I decided that it was best for me not to become disheartened by his lack of talking about it.

The next time I visited Mum was enjoyable. I was able to laugh at how she was behaving like a naughty little girl ... again. Each visit showed that her dementia was worsening, and she'd quickly become upset with my sister and me when we spoke to any of the other residents, even the residents I knew from having worked there. When she finally settled in, my sister booked her in for regular Friday comb-ups in the nursing home's hairdressing salon. My mother was pleased,

Chapter 15

but she was aging rapidly, and I was happy to have dissolved the anger I'd carried for far too long; better able to laugh off her orders that she placed on me as soon as I'd arrive.

It was sad to see her now a frail little old lady, sitting in a water chair to avoid pressure sores, her blanket over her knees and a look of confusion in her eyes. She'd know that she'd forgotten something but wasn't sure what it was. She had many skin tears and also suffered from scabies, which ravaged her body. The MRSA infection still raged in her left eye, and I truly wished I was able to move her into my home so I could care for her, but I was still having too much trouble looking after myself.

I'd become entangled in my clothing when trying to dress myself; most days having to cut my bra off after my attempt to get it on by stepping into it to pull it up. Unable to lift my arms or twist around to clip it up, when it is half on, I was then unable to get it up or down because of pain and sensitivity and balance issues, also weakness in my left side, so most times when I got it halfway on, I'd snip it off! And there were more tears! So, phones, keys, handbags, and anything I had to carry, were not the only things needing to be replaced in my life! It was still difficult to balance myself when so tired — I fell often, sometimes many times in a day.

I was pleased to be back home and see more of my girls, and I imagined they were also pleased to not have to travel to visit me way on the other side of the city. Happiest of all for me to be home was Dudley ...

Chapter 16

Recovering from my brain haemorrhage and strokes, I thought a great deal about the events I have been able to uncover and write about. I see my life in a different way; I am glad I didn't die, telling myself that everything in our lives happens exactly when and how it is meant to. If my brain damage had happened at any other time, I would have had a different outcome. I may have been driving and killed myself and my mother, and possibly another carload of innocent people. Or, worse, I may have had my grandchildren in the car and killed them! If it happened twelve hours earlier, I may have been asleep and would have never woken up.

I find that now I'm able to cuddle up to Mum, and I tell myself that it is better late than never. I comfort myself knowing I pulled a positive out of her ways, by learning to always show my children how much I love them, so they never feel unloved like I had felt. Is this why my girls have called me 'smother' instead of mother, or is this just their sense of humour? To my knowledge, they have never felt unloved — well, I hope not from me.

Chapter 16

When I visit my mother now, I feed her, and she tells me she is not so old that she needs feeding. I often remind her: 'Well, you are naughty and because you won't feed yourself, I will feed you, because if I don't feed you, you won't eat!' Which, according to her, is because she should be living with me. I then tell her that she won't be moving in with me until she shows that she is able to feed herself.

These days Mum sleeps deeply and on one occasion she was unable to be woken for feeding and a shower. After sleeping for three days, she was sent to hospital where her vitals were taken. They took blood, did scans and an MRI looking for any sign of stroke or T.I.A. She was catheterised, sleeping through all tests. Waking after two days, the doctors had no medical concern that anything was wrong, other than she was getting old and so she was sent back to the nursing home. The next day, Mum was handing orders out once again with no memory of the previous few days.

The return to our house in the shire was good, but it had an eerie feel to it, with memories returning about how unhappy I had been here before my bleed. I was very disappointed in the renovations. When it was time to select a paint colour for the outside of our house, I picked a colour I hated because nothing else was how I had wanted it to be and there was nothing I liked about everything having been changed. I was unable to tell anyone though for risk of seeming ungrateful.

The following day, Raelene invited me for a sleepover at her place because her fiancé was working so it was a good chance for us to catch up. We had a nice time together and we planned to visit Mum the next day.

The following morning, Ruby called urging me to check the death notices in the local paper. Ross; dead at 57. How do I feel? I can't say because I don't know what this feeling that sweeps over me is called! I have felt so many new feelings of late, but I don't know what this one is. A few days later, Ruby and I went to his funeral. I don't know why I went, but I was pleased to see his family again after so many years. Especially Tina and his elder sister who tried to protect me from Ross all those years ago. Sadly, most of his siblings had not turned up and I heard there had been some drama in the family caused by him. However, there was good in the family with one brother now a priest. I enjoyed seeing them again. I began to be flooded with memories from so long back, and how Ross' family cared about me more than my own did. I found out that the night at his sister's when the police couldn't find him, he had been hiding in the roof after climbing through the manhole in the bathroom!

It was now three and a half years since my brain haemorrhage. James had a new job once again, this time in Queensland and he began to stay there for a few days each week. Raelene and her fiancé moved back in with me, giving them a chance to save money and also to be on hand for me, which was a big relief for James to know I had help in the house with various repairs and pool cleaning. Although much better, I would not be able to fight off an intruder if need be, so I think James was relieved to know I had company in the house apart from Dudley.

I hated James being away but was learning to switch my hurts off and store them in my dead-wood pile, well aware I couldn't be emotionally distraught anymore. I was hurting inside when he was home for a few brief days each week. I didn't like how I felt when I was with him, but I didn't tell him this, knowing he would not understand and may have assumed I was picking a fight. My eldest grandson was about to turn twenty-one, so I planned to fly north in a few weeks to meet James and we would then travel to Toowoomba to celebrate this event, which makes me realise how the past twenty-one years have flown. We stayed for a weekend of celebrations then we returned to James' unit on the Gold Coast. Once back, he seemed anxious to get out and catch up with his new friends at the local club just down the end of the street. I was not asked, and I began to see how involved he was with his friends, and how happy he was at his new address. Apart from our trip to Toowoomba, I hadn't seen much of him because he was out on most nights. In the past when I had been there, he would take time off work to take me out but not this time, so I was aware that a lot had changed for him and I wondered if he had a girlfriend, or if he was ever going to come home. I asked him to book me a flight home the next day. 'Sure, no problem.' He seemed keen to do this for me, so I angrily thought I would never go back up there again. I didn't want to feel so unloved anymore and I didn't like how I felt when I was with him. Annoyed at his happy friends, and jealous that he wanted to be with them, I just wanted to be home in my own place where I wouldn't be a bother to him.

Once back home I was happy to be in my own environment, each day trying to swim, still with such weakness on my left side, so I was swimming lopsided, becoming perfect at swimming in arc shapes. The dreadful pain in my shoulder made coordination hard, but I was determined to do laps so I could tell Dr Chandler about it when I saw him for my yearly check-up.

I constantly tried with everything in me to become a 'repaired' person and when I was in the pool, Dudley swam with me and seemed to know how I had to be near the side in case I needed to hang on. He stopped swimming when I stopped, and I wondered what he would do if I got into any kind of trouble and began to sink. Well, I wasn't about to find out because I was well aware of my limitations and my boundaries were not to be pushed. My girls and I called Dudley 'Thorpey' when he was in the pool, because he loved to swim. One day, through my new friend, Janice, I actually met Ian Thorpe, who said he was impressed to have Dudley nicknamed after him.

Each evening, I was now in bed at six o'clock, exhausted from the efforts to improve the workings of my body. Swimming put me in a zombie state but was better to do than sitting around watching television with a remote that

Chapter 16

I was unable to work, which was often thrown across the room. I have always been very active, and I wanted to return to that person, so I took Dudley out for many walks in the park across the road.

At my next consultation with Dr Chandler, I told him I was swimming, and not just swimming in circles. 'I can now do a lap!' He seemed surprised more than anything, but I imagined he was pleased that I was able to do this. During my consultation, I once again thanked him for saving my life. After my visit, when I left his room, I told myself '365 more sleeps and I can see him again'. He was the only man interested in the things I could now do and although only from a professional interest, it encouraged me to achieve more things to tell him about. After each consultation I began to make a new goal, so I was able to tell him at my next visit. (These days I am making an effort to be happy and have made an agreement with myself to smile and say hello to people when out walking with Dudley because I don't want to be like I was in the past when I was so unhappy. I turned away from people so that I didn't have to smile and say hello. I was annoyed by happy people, but I now tell myself this is not to happen anymore!) Many things were going on my dead-wood pile and occasionally I'd sort through a few things in the pile. I was now beginning to see how James and I were losing each other and how far apart we had become — I knew we were wired differently, but in reality, I chose to not see this. I didn't want to continue living in an emotional vacuum in my need of love from James. This only caused me to ache.

Soon, I began to notice changes about myself. Some things were no longer important to me — my gardens were now too much work, and I no longer had the energy, balance or the desire to tend them. My priorities had been moved around since recently reassessing my life and I now put my own needs first. I was still getting upset when I dropped something and had many falls when I attempted to pick things up. I was still unable to wear jeans, unable to do up a button or a zipper. I couldn't wear track pants with a tie in front, still unable to tie a bow, so pull ups were worn by me for ease in dressing. After a few embarrassing times, I needed to stay aware of the fact that they may drop down, again.

James was home for a few days each week, but I was now becoming angry that even when at home, he was not at home. I hadn't told him how he had been seen in the airport the week before, so I knew he had been in town and not told me. I was curious, where did he stay? He seemed to have a secret and I was aware that in order to protect myself from further hurt, I had to let it go. On his next visit home, he told me that he had left the job up north and had bought a business from a friend in Wollongong and was moving it up north with him. Did that mean he had decided to never return to me? Was he ever coming home? Again, I wondered if he had a girlfriend up there. But if I wanted to be a well-adjusted person then it was high time for me to realise that I was once again becoming unhappy with my curious thoughts. I wouldn't turn to alcohol as I had done in the past and I told myself to not box things up. I needed to get out of my own way, just let go! Stop looking for answers!

Dudley became concerned when he saw me cry, and I realised that this dog had the emotions of a human ... well, some humans. I tried to remain positive by remembering how lucky I was to be alive, so I was not going to let myself down with the emotions that had hurt me in the past when I had allowed myself to live like an emotional fool. I was going to be strong now and realise that I was no longer in James' world.

Soon he began to not answer my calls, so our talks on the phone were no longer happening at all. I was told by his family to not worry because he was busy and most probably out of range, therefore unable to use his phone. Well, how come I can phone Ireland? That would be out of range more than the next state! His youngest brother moved up north to assist James by working with him in his business. So, there was my answer — it seemed he had no intention of returning to me and was permanently up north.

Chapter 17

I didn't want to remain hurt from my situation with James or frustrated with my body's inabilities and pain in my shoulder. When I over-thought, it seemed to result in bad days, and I'd become aware of losing my sense of self, as if I didn't occupy my own body and was living outside of it. Also, feeling that I needed to move forward confidently and that there was a greater power running through my life, I decided to attend church each Sunday morning, well aware that my father would not approve.

Was I losing sense of who I was? I suffered from an occasional migraine, which scared the shit out of me. I worried it was leading to another bleed, even though it was just an ache and not a strong pain like the freight train I had felt in my head before my bleed. On my next consultation I told Dr Chandler, who assured me that the pain wasn't associated with any brain bleed, and as I had complete faith in him, I was no longer concerned. I just wanted them to stop, so I told myself not to let my fears rule my head and to let go of the emotions that had hurt me in the past.

Chapter 17

The following Sunday was my first attendance in church. The walk there was all uphill, and with my twisted body that tires so easily, I was soon in zombie mode. In church, I began to hear people singing. On waking, I realised everyone was leaving and I wondered what was happening. Why is everyone leaving? Where are they going? Mass had ended and I'd slept through the entire hour. I tried sneaking out before anyone I knew had seen me, but of course this was impossible and when someone spoke to me, I was lucky that he and his wife knew me. They were amused when I asked them where everyone was going. They told me how funny it was that they had heard me snoring during the service, as apparently, I had slept through it all. I decided that the next attendance would be better because I would leave home with plenty of time for a slow walk so as to not wear myself out.

The following week, just as I was about to leave, it began raining very heavily. Maybe I should have stayed home, but it was Palm Sunday, the anniversary of my father's death. I wondered — was his spirit trying to keep me from going with all the rain pelting? But I decided that this was silly, and using my umbrella, I walked uphill against the rain. On arrival, the church was packed. I was in zombie mode again, and with nowhere to sit, I walked along the back wall, supporting my tired body as I gingerly progressed by leaning on the wall with my hand. I leaned too hard on the wall that turned out to be a door and suddenly, with a very loud bang, I fell into a room for toddlers and parents, shocking all in there, not to mention the entire congregation who had all turned to see me being helped to my feet by a man holding his now-screaming baby. Due to the pain in my left shoulder and weakness in my left side, I was still unable to get to my feet without help, so the man helped me with my entire body weight being involved.

Now quite aware that I may not be as well as I had first thought, I wrote a letter of apology to the priest. The following Sunday's Mass brought more glares when I dropped the collection bowl with all the money tipping out onto the floor. What a loud noise with the clatter of coins rolling everywhere — *me again*! I thought it may be a better option for me to attend Mass on Saturday afternoons when no one would know me, thinking also that I'd need to be careful walking home in the dark.

Many years prior, James' mother had provided a few snippets to me of the Catholic religion and faith as she had gone through the process of christening me and had briefly explained the background. This had fuelled my curiosity then and even more so when on the following Saturday I set out for church, looking forward to learning about Joseph and Mary. I had no knowledge they were parents to Jesus and was slowly piecing it all together in my mind. I'd worked myself into a dither though, wondering if I should've attended church at all. Nervously, I sat at the end of the aisle so as not to be in a position to have to grab the money bowl with my left hand (in case I dropped it again). At that end I could use my right hand, which worked well.

Chapter 17

I noticed that the couple sitting in front of me was Mum's doctor and her husband. This was the doctor who I had seen with my head pain and who had sent me for many tests. I had seen her a few weeks prior and told her about my mother now being in the nursing home where I had worked so I asked her if she'd be able to drop in for a visit. She said she would be happy to visit Mum, just as she had been to see me in hospital, although I had no memory of her doing so. I thought maybe she had visited after an outing in hospital when I returned from rehab in zombie mode. Feeling like a real church person though, I turned my attention to the service that was just beginning.

Unfortunately, I was shattered when the person next to me began shaking me vigorously. Wondering what on earth was wrong with her to shake me, to my horror, I realised I'd fallen asleep again, and worse — had begun to snore loudly. Embarrassed, at the end of the service I again tried to sneak away before I was seen by anyone, but my heart sank when I heard someone call out asking me if I wanted a lift home. All eyes on me, I accepted the lady's kind offer and on the way home I told her about falling into the parents' room some weeks before! Oh yes, she had heard all about that she confirmed with a smile, and although she thought it was funny, she had admired my strength and determination.

Each Saturday or Sunday, rain or shine, I attended church, and my long walks there were draining, placing me in zombie mode every week, but I persisted. Along the way, I would exercise my memory by selecting any day out of the past week and I tried to remember what it was that I did on that day. So, on most days when I arrived at the church, I was not only physically exhausted but also mentally worn out, so little wonder that I was usually ready for a sleep!

I was pleased to learn about the life and times of Jesus, but the only thing I don't like about church was that I was unable to take Dudley. After church and my marathon walk back home, and my sleep, followed by lunch, I'd then walk to the club not far from home to catch up with friends who had been so good to me when I was first out of hospital. Each had brought meals or helped in the garden, cleaned my home, brought washing in, toileted me and sometimes my friends would take me out to lunch. I remembered all they had done for me, and I appreciated having such kind friends, so I often saw them at the club. Of course, Dudley used to go with me, all my friends knowing that he was a human dog! Dudley was always such good company for me, particularly with the ongoing problem of James' absence with the new business and not answering my calls. I still wondered if he had a girlfriend but decided for sanity' sake I did not dwell on it.

On a very hot Sunday while getting ready for church, Dudley dropped his lead in front of me for a walk. He had no knowledge that he was a dog and hadn't mastered reading a clock, so he didn't know it was time for me to head off. I promised him we'd walk and have a swim when I got back home, also saying that we'd visit his Staffy friend Rex, who lived nearby. I was lucky enough to get a lift home on that dreadfully hot day. On my arrival home, I was unable to open the front door, because Dudley was laying closely behind. After some time trying to put my arm into a slim opening, I encouraged him to move so I could get inside. Something was terribly wrong — he wasn't happy with excitement as usual, instead, he looked sad and dark in his eyes, going into the bathroom and pawing behind the toilet system where a tiny mouse wouldn't fit. Many years previously, when I had my Great Danes, I had read books on dog psychology, so I became concerned knowing a dog will go looking for a place to die. I checked his pulse which was normal, but his temperature was high. I gave him ice and put cold water on him. He hadn't improved an hour later and began to salivate and to have diarrhoea. Concerned that he was dehydrated, or his body was shutting down, I phoned the vet again who said to try to get him there as soon as possible. Joanne had been upstairs sleeping after a night out with friends and we were able to get him onto his trampoline bed and into the back of her car. He was looking at me with such darkness in his eyes. Joanne reassured me, telling me to talk normally to him because Dudley was able to sense my feelings. I wanted his tail to move like it always did, recalling how James would say that Dudley's tail was like his heart, it just pumped on and on, and if ever Dudley stopped wagging his tail, he would die. Now, for the first time ever, his tail was so still ...

On arrival at the vet's rooms, it was like a scene from E.R.; a vet came to the car to help us take him inside where he was checked over and showered with cold water. This was an attempt to cool him down from the car trip, which had overheated him. I was told to return home and wait for a call. I wanted to stay with Dudley, knowing he would miss me if I left him — we were always together, he was my friend — the one who heard it all. So, I waited for him to fall asleep before Joanne took me home.

Once back home, I began praying for him to get better. I had broken sleep that night, waking sick in the morning.

Then came the phone call to tell me of his death. I felt like I had lost a part of me. My best mate was gone. I felt so empty and alone knowing he wouldn't be coming home today.

What would I do without him? I hoped he hadn't been in pain or afraid without me and I thought that he must have been looking for me when he was so close to the door. Joanne rang her sisters and soon, many calls came. My sister arrived and asked could she phone James, to which I firmly replied NO, although unfortunately Raelene had already phoned James' mother who naturally would have told him. Losing Dudley was not something I could deal with then or at any time — emotionally unstable and feeling so alone, my world felt as though a big hole had been ripped in it and I wished this wasn't happening.

News spread about Dudley and soon friends begin ringing. I was even getting flowers by delivery. A few hours later, James rang one of my daughters to say that he would be down to see me and though he was told that I didn't want this, a few hours later he arrived and couldn't understand why I didn't want him there, telling me that he hadn't answered my calls because it was what I had wanted!

Where did he get that idea from? I was no longer afraid to tell him how I felt so I let him know that I thought he had a girlfriend. He said that I was just picking a fight and being silly and he put his arms around me. I wanted to push him away and hit him! I *knew* he would put his arms around me, thinking it was all I needed to make things better. Did he think it was okay that he chose not to answer my calls? Although I knew Dudley's death would upset him, I wanted James to go.

Later that night he rang to ask me to go back up north with him, saying I needed to get out of the house. Although I refused, he was able to get my daughters to convince me, so I went.

This time, after a couple of days of again not seeing much of James, I wanted to be back home with my daughters and friends who *did* care. When I asked him to book a return flight for me, again there was no hesitation, and it was done that same day.

On the way to the airport, I told James I would never return because with his new friends, I had felt distant from him. I also told him I was annoyed with them being so friendly and how they told me things about him! He was mine, not theirs, and I didn't need them to tell me about James; their closeness annoyed me. Did they know we had been together over twenty-one years? We had history, had he not told them that? I was jealous, and this time it had hurt me too much. I felt alienated.

I was glad to be home and told my daughters I had the worst time possible and was never going back. Monday came and I went to see my friend Georgia to tell her about my awful week, and how I felt James had a girlfriend. Her response was the same as that of my family, saying James wouldn't do that to me because he was a man of principle. In my heart I knew they were right; he was not a woman-chaser.

That same day I visited Mum to tell her about Dudley's death. She held my hand and gave me comfort, and for the first time I can recall, I didn't pull away from her, letting her stroke my hand (her way of showing concern). I was able to accept her expression of warmth. I wondered ... had I softened after walking past her house, school yard and church? She showed me more comfort over Dudley's death than she had shown to me when my son had died many years ago.

I started to get out of the house that I now hated every part of. I was out early and home late, some days just going on train rides alone so as not to be hard work for anyone who felt the need to comfort me. I was aware that I was no longer a part of James' world, nor was he a part of mine. Though we hadn't spoken about separation, it was obvious he had no intention of moving back home and I wondered why he couldn't tell me as much. I felt like the world outside was locked from me and strongly felt like I was in a pit. I walked for hours. Occasionally I was called 'Forrest' when friends saw me walking all over the place when they drove past, because Forrest Gump walked for three months. I imagined that this was better than being called a 'cry baby' ...

Chapter 18

Now that I no longer had Dudley, I visited my mother daily. This pleased her and I enjoyed being able to do some volunteer work there. This gave me a feel of self-worth and helped the day pass. My mother needed to see an eye specialist on account of the MRSA infection in her left eye, which was resisting all antibiotics and appeared to have taken up residency. My sister and I were told by the eye specialist that our mother was to be admitted into a ward at the eye hospital for possible surgery. Due to the MRSA, she was kept in a room completely on her own. All visitors had to glove and gown up when visiting her because she was also covered in a rash, diagnosed as scabies. She had developed this even while on antibiotics for the eye infection. I felt that she had been taking antibiotics for so long, she had developed antibiotic resistance. It was so sad to watch her scratching her fine skin that tore like thin rice paper. The infection was so stubborn that the doctors resorted to a partial cornea transplant, and she was kept in the eye hospital for a month.

Back in the nursing home, Mum told us how pleased

she was to return, which was also a great relief to us. Most days, my girls visited her and painted her nails in shades of her favourite purple and lilac colours. Once again, she was sleeping for days at a time with no memory of doing so and would wake only to start raving about past events from years ago, as though they happened yesterday. She also talked about things she'd dreamt as though they had been actual events in her life, which with my obscure dreams, I could draw a parallel. Having this in common, I could understand her delusions and ravings to a point, as well as the inability to distinguish them from reality.

With her prolonged sleep pattern, we were fearful that one day she may not wake up, and this continued for many months, in and out of sleep for days at a time. I was glad I'd been able to move on from the rejection felt from her as a child (and carried for far too long), now able to hold her hand and talk to comfort her.

James had been down to take me out to breakfast, and I picked up that he wanted to tell me something, but he didn't know how to. I felt he was a little on edge and irritated, so I decided to make it easy for him. I needed to know, so I asked him again if he had a girlfriend. Annoyed, he asked why I always had to start a fight and angrily told me he didn't approve of me always asking.

I still had suspicions, but later that day, when Georgia assured me that he wouldn't have a girlfriend, I assumed I must have been wrong. 'He wouldn't be interested in another woman. He is a man of principle, and he just likes to be with mates and buy them drinks.' It was important to James to be liked by his mates, and over the years, I had often felt that he wanted to please them more than me. Georgia was right, she'd worked in our business long enough to know him well, so I tried to dismiss the thoughts and replaced my concerns by looking forward to my next visit to Dr Chandler, realising that I'd more than likely be going on my own.

I didn't imagine James would come because when he came home, he now stayed with a mate around the corner and not in our home with me. I didn't know why, but I assumed he just wanted to be away from me, although he stated that it was how I wanted it to be. I thought a lot about the heated conversation we'd had on the way to the airport after my visit, and recalled telling him if he had a girlfriend, she wouldn't love him as much as I did. James had been unhappy with that comment.

My next visit to Dr Chandler was unsurprisingly alone and it was four years since my bleed. He seemed surprised that I had travelled alone by train to see him. I thought it best not to mention James, assuming he was only interested in my brain and its workings. My emotional pain was another matter though, so I did tell him about Dudley's death. Dr Chandler told me when his family lost their pet dog it was a sad event for all and that he knew how I felt, but I don't think anyone knew how sad my heart really was, especially now with all of my suspicions.

Dr Chandler asked me many things and I suspect he may have been checking my cognitive abilities and how fast I processed answers. I don't think he was really interested to know what I did each day! I told him that when I was sad, I'd catch a train and go all over the place to keep myself busy — I didn't want anyone to think I needed cheering up.

With Dudley gone to doggy heaven, I now told Georgia all my fears and hurts. She was such a good friend and good company for me, and we laughed a lot. She had Fridays off work, so we'd spend the day together shopping for bargains in all the local op shops. Through the week she'd bring me meals for dinner. She was the only person I told how much I hated the house and my hurt at being unable to have the style I'd wanted. I needed to get out each day and get away from the house, which I hated.

Dudley had been gone for six months and I looked forward to seeing my mother most days. We were once again laughing together, and I found happiness in her company. Mum's dementia seemed to help her find some happiness, and there was no more bossing anyone around, me included, so I enjoyed these times. Ruby and Anne also visited her as did Jenny, who often spoke to her about the many nights going to clubs together and how she could out-dance most!

I hadn't heard from James in a few months, and I was

curious, knowing he'd again been in town and not called me. Reluctantly, I realised I'd been right about him no longer wanting me in his life. Mum often asked about James, especially after I had to told her about my suspicions.

At ninety-two, Mum, who was always so well-groomed and glamorous (and loving the camera) was unaware of her now aging body, perhaps a product of the progressing dementia. I felt lucky to still have her and I enjoyed her long overdue affection towards me. She was still doing the sleep marathons much too often though and I grew concerned, having watched the rapid decline of other aged residents during the time I worked at the home. I decided that the next time it happened would be the time to get my eldest daughter to come down from Toowoomba. My sister said she would get her son to also come down from Brisbane; both of us afraid our mother was slipping away.

Our children arrived for a visit, which Mum peacefully slept through. So, after three days our kids returned home. Mum woke two days later not knowing anything about the past five days, or our fears! A month later when it happened again, there was understandable hesitance from her grandchildren, who could not return ...

Sadly, a week after our children returned to their homes, our mother at ninety-three stopped breathing. Taken by angels in her sleep like someone blessed ... fearing nothing.

When my father was alive, they had both filled in the paperwork required to have their body taken to the medical university after death, for medical learning. My father had gone thirty-five years previously, and Frank and I placed his ashes in the surf at Cronulla Beach.

I was pleased I'd made peace with myself over my mother's treatment of me when I was little, and I was very glad to have been able to release a lot of hurt that I had carried for far too long. A few months later, Mum's ashes were ready to be picked up. So, the following Mother's Day was the day we chose to put her ashes in the Nuns' Pool where we had spent many happy days together. We hoped she'd be reunited with our father at sea, only about two hundred metres away. My sister brought along our nanna's ashes too, which Mum had kept, and her ashes were put at sea with her daughter. We released purple balloons into the sky on an unusually warm, sunny day. I had told my girls not to worry, as my dad would organise a nice sunny day, with a high tide and no other people around. This was seemingly an impossibility, especially at that time of year, so I'd also warned of rain and cold. I was surprised but so glad that Dad and Mother Nature had provided a warm, sunny day. We all paid for a plaque, which was mounted on the rock wall overlooking the rock pool.

In the days and weeks following, when I was a little down, I'd take a cut lunch and sit with her plaque. In my mind's eye I could see us both here with my girls, all enjoying the ocean. I would think back of the days with her, and I'd feel her with me. I'd recall her love of bright colours, her love of music, her dance stamina, and how she adored her pin-up boy — Engelbert Humperdinck!

I was glad she was unaware of her deteriorating body, her dribbling and her rapid decline. Instead, I reflected on the image of us back then and I see us all there together, the girls happily swimming in the rock pool. After her death I was glad to have had the extra time needed to be able to put together a fitting eulogy, which was hard work with my mind still unable to retain much. My sister also wrote a tribute, as did Leigh and her sisters, beginning with: 'To the best and most loving grandmother in the world!'

I was so proud of their ability to put words together so beautifully, and included in their memories were many of Mum's funny little sayings. Leigh spoke with such loyalty and love, and I felt so proud of her. My dear friend Ruby also wrote something beautiful to this woman who had played nanna to her first child. My mother was much loved by all who knew her. My sister and I asked all who came to wear bright colours. We wore purple, knowing Mum would especially want this; in fact, expect it. If she was able to see the day, she would've been quite touched with the tributes and the moving DVD made by Raelene, which included Mum's most loved (pop) music. She would have loved all the fuss, and as always, would have loved being guest of honour, with her favourite singer — Engelbert Humperdinck — singing her most loved songs.

My biggest surprise on the day came when I saw a woman and was curious of her face but unable to place it. She approached me and said hello and I knew this voice — it was

Fuzzy Wuzzy, Kris from my childhood. Kris had moved away, no one knowing where to. It had been over forty years, but Jenny had found her. Sadly, there had been no conversation between us for a few years, but now we were all together at my mother's farewell. Fuzzy Wuzzy and I have since stayed in touch.

I missed my mother every day, wishing I could laugh with her again. Her death was a major turning point in my life. James turned up at the service and this was the first time I had seen him or been in a position to speak to him for seven months. I will never understand why he did not ring or send me a text message when my mother passed away. At least, on this day, he turned up, but with our long history I found this difficult to understand, unable to get my head around the nothing at all from him — no words, no comfort or card, yet he did bring flowers to her service. That was so not at all like him, and I was hurt that he couldn't even speak to me. What on earth had I done so wrong? Maybe I asked him too many times did he have a girlfriend? At the service he didn't come near me, so I went to him and said, 'Thanks for coming and thanks for the lovely flowers.'

'That's okay,' James mumbled.

I don't know when he left or who with — he never said goodbye. I didn't hear from James until six weeks later a text message came for my birthday ... I deleted it! Two years before this on Christmas Day he had called into Marie's house on the way to his family. He wanted to talk about how we would have to sell the house. I was unable to have this conversation with him. I was overwhelmed with sadness when he left because he was going to see his family. I didn't want my children to know how much I wished I was also going to see them. We hadn't been a couple for a year so, again, I wasn't asked. It seemed that nothing much had changed for James, aside from his address, and we didn't speak, except for a text message through cyber space. For me there had been big changes since my bleed, not only with James' move away, but also with the deaths of Dudley and Mum.

Every day had taken on a new feeling for me, and I was so alone in the house that I hated. I could have slipped into depression, but I was not about to let that happen, so I made an effort to get out every day. With no mother to visit and no Dudley, I felt great sadness and fought to keep it from consuming me. James had mentioned selling the house, so I expected it was going to happen soon, it was inevitable now, especially with him in another state so far away and so much distance between us. I tried to convince myself I didn't really care. I truly didn't like the house anymore, there was nothing I liked about the renovations, so I didn't need to convince myself.

I was curious about where my life was headed. I was unable to hold down a job in a body that wouldn't work properly, so I would have no income. Where would I live? What on? Sadly, I thought about when we had moved into the house, and I had made it my home by painting walls and covering the lounge. I made curtains for each room and spent hours in the gardens, making the place look pretty. All these years later and after the events of the previous five years, I would be more than happy to part with this huge place. I consoled myself in knowing that my dislike would only make it easier to part with it. I would not allow myself to feel saddened and would accept all the changes and move forward with no regrets.

I kept busy each day going for walks. No Dudley meant, sadly, I now walked alone, but I solved everything, at least in my head. I could solve all the world problems! This was better than being absorbed in my own dramas. Thursdays I was still meeting with Janice for our walks, but our walks are sometimes across the Harbor Bridge or through the city. On Fridays, I'd still go out with Georgia, and I had my mornings at the gym, also my yoga classes and a weights class, which was probably another reason why I slept fourteen hours each night. I had the occasional girlie day out with friends and spent great times with Ruby and Anne, so my life was full and active, which helped me to stay positive. Weekends were usually spent with my children, so I was busy each day.

Although still seeing James' family, as I was a godmother to a niece, I tried to put James in my past. A few months later, a friend of ours died and James called to say he would pick me up to attend the funeral. It felt strange when he picked me up because we hadn't spoken over the past few months except for the time he again mentioned having to sell our home. Each time he had flown home, he stayed around the corner at a mate's place.

When he picked me up, not much was said between us and at our friend's funeral, we didn't spend time together, instead, we talked to many others at the wake. Afterwards, he dropped me home with the comment, 'We need to sell the house.'

I wanted to say, yes, yes, you have been saying that for the past eighteen months, but I didn't. In the morning, James rang to say he had listed our house with an agent. I felt things were really coming to an end for us and I was upset that he listed the house for sale without me. I felt we should have done this together because the house was OUR house, not just his! I had heard that it needed to be sold because his business was not doing well.

Our house was soon sold, and I was given six weeks to pack up and move out. I had reached a phase in my life knowing I had to let go of James, so I reminded myself I was never able to make him happy, so what did I expect? Now, it was obvious he would continue with his life up north with his new friends, completely unaware how my life made no sense to me without him in it. My life had changed so much over the past few years; I felt like a different person. I knew I needed to be happy and that this was entirely up to me. I am accountable for my own happiness, I'd remind myself!

I refused to ache over James anymore and decided to rid myself of him while packing. In order to achieve this, I would have to throw away all the things he had bought me over the years. In a few weeks, I had packed everything; all James' things were in the garage, ready for him to collect. I didn't want to be there when he arrived, so I rang Georgia, who came to pick me up and I spent the day with her.

Over the following weeks, I cleaned the entire house. Georgia called in daily to take car loads away. After five weeks our house was barren and empty. My furniture was now stored in a friend's garage and James had taken some to his home in Queensland. I feel sad when I compare the time that we moved in with that moment and all that had happened since. For the next few days, I lived out of a suitcase and slept on a single bed mattress on the floor in this (destroyed, as far as I was concerned) pit of a house. I was glad of having only five days left to live in the hell hole, but I became consumed with many feelings.

I was physically burnt out after spending each day packing, cleaning and carting unwanted goods to charity shops; every day now I was in zombie mode because I had worked my body too hard. My body tired so fast, and I was soon aching from head to toe, and with limited balance, I was having many falls. I was emotionally torn and carrying curious thoughts of James and his new life away from me. The last thing left to do was to clean the walls. While doing this, a feeling of faintness washed over me ... I collapsed. When I woke, I had no knowledge of how long I had been on the floor, and while looking for my phone, began to be sick. I was unable to get onto my feet, so I crawled into my bedroom, sick with a thumping headache, but relieved to get my hands on my phone. I rang my sister who came straight away and took me to her place to care for me, saying I had '… been through enough' and that she would see I would 'go through no more'.

I was bursting on all levels, not knowing how to deal with so many emotions that I wasn't ready for. Where do I start? I had always been a person to take ownership of my problems and deal with any issues, so I told myself I would deal with this. I didn't know how, but I would. I wouldn't let any of this break me. I had been given a second chance at life, and I was also realising that over the past years I had allowed my emotions to break me. Now, I would gain knowledge from the feelings. I would *not* allow my soul to be sucked out by anyone, *ever* again. The following day, Raelene picked me up from my sister's place to take me back to the house and help finish the cleaning up. We then took the key to the agents — goodbye house!

I moved into my sister's place and although my head was in a dark place, I knew this would pass. But I couldn't shake the feeling of now being with no home of my own — a homeless person, one with very little self-esteem and no self-worth, unable to work and totally broken down in every area. My next challenge was to repair myself, mostly emotionally, and I was determined to achieve this!

While living with my sister, we were at last developing a long overdue relationship, something we never had. Now that we were both grown women, we should enjoy becoming close to each other. I appreciated her helping me and over the following weeks we became good friends, discussing times that each other didn't know about. We had grown up with great distance between us. The five years between us had given us different experiences, different friends, and of course, different personalities. During that time, I tried to close all areas involving James, knowing I needed to do this in order to move out of this bleak head space that had taken over me.

I was finding myself now immersed in church each Sunday morning and, good for me, *not* falling asleep and missing out on anything… I was familiar with many faces there, and I hoped they had forgotten I was the one who fell through the back wall in church, dropped the collection tray, and occasionally fell asleep snoring quite loudly! While at my sister's, I attended church with a little old lady living in the same block. She was very nice, but sadly, had myeloma, a bone marrow disease, so I gave her my mother's walking frame.

Close to the end of six weeks, I found a little unit in the shire a short walk from my sister's, and I felt something nice when I was shown inside. I loved how perfect it was for me and felt like it had been waiting for me. I wondered if my mother's spirit guided me there. To be only a few blocks away from the house I had grown up in, and which I had later purchased with Frank, and where our daughters had grown up, all seemed a bit too pat. Before moving into my own place, I went for a walk past my parents' house and I recalled my childhood with the yelling, the smashing and the beltings.

These memories brought unsettling feelings, like looking back into another life. That night, I had a bad dream, so I decided to stay away from my childhood house until my head was in a better place. I had all my areas in repair mode, so I didn't need to focus on anything except myself for a while.

July sixth arrived, and I was given the key to my little home. I have heard a saying, *Once a shire girl always a shire girl*, which sure applies to me now. This was the best I had felt for quite some time. I was happy and confident that nothing was going to let me down, so it may have been a good thing that I no longer heard from James, except for one occasion. We met at the solicitor's office to sign mortgage papers for my unit, which James had promised to pay off for me. It was no small thing for him to do, but the officialness of it rocked me and irked me at the same time. He asked if I was looking forward to moving.

'No, I'm sad the way things have turned out.'

James told me that I was lucky to have my own place because he had to move into a mate's place and share rent, adding, 'At least you will have privacy.'

When the day arrived for my move, I heard church bells ringing from the church only two blocks away. This was the church where Frank and I were married. Ironically, that day would've been our fortieth wedding anniversary and here I was moving into a unit of my own. I had much history behind me that I didn't want to let come into my head. I couldn't help but wonder where I would be had I stayed in the marriage that I had been so happy in until our son died, and things then went downhill ... I am *not* to think about that, not that day, so I pushed on with my move, exhausted, but reminding myself how lucky I was to have repaired with a second chance at life. I was also well enough to be able to do most of the move on my own, even though while moving I was soon in zombie mode ... but I was happy!

It was planned that my son-in-law and a grandson would help with the heavy things the next day. Over the following few weeks, I felt happiness and a comfort in my new home, realising that home is no longer a place to pretty up, but a place where the only thing I need to feel is safe and secure. So, when friends asked how I was, I spoke honestly, telling them I was well and happy. They'd reply how nice it was to see me smile. When out walking, I was able to look people in the eye and say hello; a thing I was unable to do when I was so unhappy. I have learnt that a person can be with someone they love, yet at the same time, they can be so very lonely.

While settling into my new home, I no longer had feelings of worthlessness. When November arrived, the days were warming up and I was curious why James still wouldn't respond to any text message sent to him. Why couldn't he even do that? I wondered a lot about him. What was he doing? Why wouldn't he respond? I became concerned and I worried he may be sad because I know he would've hated to move into a mate's small unit and share everything. I thought he may be out drinking, but I told myself, things have changed. I am *not* to worry over a man who can't answer my phone calls and is so obviously *not* worried about me!

Larger thoughts popped up such as: Why should *I* be worrying? After all, isn't it *me* who had the brain bleed? He is still able to hold down a job, drive a car, fly around in a plane — isn't it *me* whose life and body had been shut down in so many areas? I can't do anything much now. It's hard to hold a conversation or hold down a job, and I'm even unable to drive. Shouldn't it be *him* concerned for *me*?

Only recently, being seven years since my bleed, have I become strong enough to live alone, unassisted and only occasionally having falls, yet James doesn't seem to wonder how *I* am managing. So, my mind once again opens up to the probability that maybe James does have a girlfriend and can't tell me. I feel torn, surprised because he does have enough respect for me to tell me. Deep down I know he has ...

Still obsessing, and in my usual style, I began to ask his mates about 'his girlfriend', hoping to find out in a tricky way, but not wanting to undo all the hard work I've done. I told myself to *stop* being such an obsessive person, or at least only obsess over the right things ...

Chapter 19

Walking to church from my home is now no longer uphill and my walk takes me past the School of Arts hall. I remember concerts there when I was a little girl, and the shyness I experienced with the big crowds that had truly terrified me. I found relief in the dressing up, thinking people wouldn't know who I was when dressed as Little Miss Muffet or Snow White! I had also won many physical culture competitions in the hall and Mum had been proud to tell everyone I was her daughter. All my medals and certificates with other treasures are stored under my bed in the suitcase my father had taken to war along with treasures from my children.

Each Saturday afternoon this same hall was transferred into a cinema, usually showing two movies. Sometimes, if I had been a good girl through the week, I was allowed to go with Robbie and Paul. I will never forget that Saturday, when the movie *Psycho* played, and I had tried to escape by hiding under the seat. It was in the days before classification and had left me screaming in fear for my life over the shower-stabbing scene.

In later years, on a Saturday night, the hall became a dance hall, and for me, had taken on a completely different feel. We danced a new dance called The Stomp. I was fifteen and I looked forward to going there with Brenda, my friend from primary school. At interval on these nights, some of us girls would walk up to the hotel to buy a bottle of Resch's Pilsener beer (then costing three and sevenpence halfpenny) requested for Barry Gibb, the older boy in the Bee Gees. I liked The Stomp because a girl didn't have to hold hands with a boy — we only had to face each other and stomp one foot, then the other — easy! My father said it wasn't real dancing, but it was for us! It *must* have been a real dance because there were songs about The Stomp called *Stomping at Maroubra* and *He's My Blond Headed Stompie Wompie Real Gone Surfer Boy*, to name a couple. These are some of the many memories that rushed in, leaving me with a strange feeling when I passed this hall.

Over time, I reached an acceptance of sorts about not hearing from James and I no longer allowed myself to focus on him. I also didn't feel like I had failed when I was unable to do much with my body, and except for the occasional curious thoughts, I was beginning to carry a calmness. My efforts to accept change in my life must have paid off because my friends began to tell me it was nice to see me happy and smiling. I'd reply: 'I have a different life now — my unit is tiny, and I have no room, I have no mother, no money, no dog, no James, yet I couldn't be happier!' With this acceptance, I tried not to fixate on any loss and realised that James and

Chapter 19

I had lost each other, and life was showing me that I was accountable for my own happiness. I learned a lot from loving James; some good, other lessons not so good. I told myself not to allow my emotions to hold me hostage and that they were not to dishearten me or my future.

I had become a more stable person, having no more emotional landslides, and my continuous self-therapy sessions while out walking seemed to be doing me some good. I settled into my new home and was happy, experiencing a familiar old feeling. It was the same feeling I felt when I was a little girl escaping to my cubby house, safe in my own little part of the world. With the return of these feelings, I realised I hadn't experienced this sense of belonging since childhood.

Five and half years since my bleed and there was much excitement in the air with Christmas Day fast approaching. It would be the first Christmas without my mother and Dudley, and I knew it would be especially hard, as most likely I also wouldn't hear from James. Although I loved the twinkly lights and the happiness on children's faces, I hated the carols, which caused me to think a lot more of my little boy. I reminded myself not to let my girls know how much I ached inside; it wasn't what they needed to hear, and I knew they'd also be missing my mother. I was determined to have a nice day.

That fifth year I was physically stronger with much better balance, and I didn't fear falling as much. My emotional balance also began to improve, and I was going forward, so I decided to show my girls how well I was doing both physically and emotionally by not pouring my heart out to them. I would brave the day!

That Christmas Day, I was picked up by my new friend — my sister — and we were off to another friend's house, who lived on the water, to have a sausage sizzle breakfast, after which, we would all pass out gifts to Santa when he did the rounds by boat to the water front homes. After that, it was off to Marie's home for lunch, then to James' family to give gifts to his nieces and nephews. I had been missing them so I thought it would be good to catch up with them all. I had only seen James' mother a few weeks prior, after she returned from having a holiday at James' place up north. I was upset, knowing that I had to try and put them all behind me. I was looking forward to the visit with James' family, whom I knew would also want to see me happy. That Christmas Day was so different to the party days when James and I were together in our house. We always had a house full of family and friends, with music and an all-day party of drinking, dancing and swimming. Almost by ritual, my friends always made a fuss over Mum, knowing how she loved the attention.

For the first time in many years, I woke alone. When my sister arrived, I let myself down by getting on a roll about James, telling her I thought he had a girlfriend. My sister knew he wouldn't because he didn't care for women. *Oh gosh, I knew she was right as Georgia had told me the same.* We set out for Fay and Greg's home and on arrival it was nice to see

Chapter 19

all our friends gathered for a Christmas breakfast. I dismissed the memory of James and I turning up together on previous Christmas Days.

While having breakfast, one of the wives told me that she and her husband had been up north and spent time with James and his new girlfriend. *WHAT*? I tried to stay composed and not show any reaction, but my stomach began churning and I needed the toilet urgently.

Unable to get the news out of my head, a range of questions whizzed around my brain. Why hadn't he told me? Why did he bite my head off whenever I asked him? Why tell me that I was trying to start a fight with him? Why this, why that? He must have thought that there was no need to tell me and obviously the friend who mentioned it assumed I knew, of course.

More questions inundated me, and I wondered at the dwindling level of respect that remained after twenty-one years together. Is this the reason he stopped answering my calls to him? Was he with her when I rang? Is that why he didn't answer? Why did he deny it when I asked? I saw then where James' loyalties lay — with her, which was why he'd stayed with a mate around the corner when he came to town. Does he think I am not worthy of telling? What about our history? Does it mean *nothing* to him? Feeling sick to my stomach and needing the toilet again, and then throwing up, I wanted to go somewhere and scream but had to maintain my composure and act normal. HOW? Soon my mind opened up to the likelihood of James turning up with her at his mother's place a bit later on the day.

I had to leave! With my insides swirling, I needed to leave so that I didn't make a fool of myself. The same friend who had dropped the information asked if I was okay and with a ripple effect, other friends asked too. I tried to get a hold of myself because I worried that the friend who told me may have realised her gaff. I explained that it was my first Christmas without Mum and Dudley and that I was a little emotional.

On the way to Marie's, I told my sister of my discovery, who said it wouldn't be true; James wouldn't do that to me. We arrived, and when Raelene arrived, I asked her to phone James to find out if it was true and if he was coming to his mother's place. Yes, it was true and I was relieved to hear that he was bringing her to meet the family the following day and I'd be able to dodge that unpleasant situation.

Oh *shit*, I hurt so deeply, but I wanted to go and see his family. Before going, I rang my family in Toowoomba to wish them a happy Christmas. One of my grandsons told me in conversation that he had had breakfast with James who told him he had moved into a mate's place with a boarder.

'Yes, I know, and he's not happy about sharing. Did you meet the boarder, what is he like?' I probed. My grandson said he thought it was a HER and her name is Mary. I didn't have to be a brain surgeon to know that this meant he was living with this new girlfriend.

My stomach felt like it was going to fall out of me again

and many things began to make sense, like a few times when he came to stay in town and told me he stayed with a mate around the corner because it was how I wanted it to be. Now I see that his loyalties were with a woman he had moved into his life. I also see why he never answered a call from me. Oh God, how would I get through the day? I began to cry so I sat in the house so as not to be seen by my other grandchildren. James' words echoed in my mind; according to him, I ended it because I had said I wasn't going up there anymore. Is that all it took for him — a brief conversation on the way to the airport? Does he think all the history we had together can be ended in a ten-minute talk on the way to the airport? I wondered then if James had no depth. I was over James' version of the truth, which were in reality only half truths. I wondered how I would handle being with his family. They would all know, and had known all along, now protecting him.

On arrival at James' family gathering, I felt despair and embarrassment. I am red eyed from crying but trying to appear normal. James' mother seemed very concerned, and I think a little embarrassed because she had stayed with James recently for a holiday, and clearly, Mary and James were then living together. I understood her not telling me, after all James is her son and blood is thicker than water. I know how a mother carries deep love for her child, despite any wrong he or she may have done.

In the past, I have often felt proud that we women are capable of feeling so many emotions in the one moment, but I was struggling with this situation. I decided to be like Scarlett O'Hara and said to myself, *Fiddle-dee-dee, I'll think about it tomorrow.* My chest was aching like it had a hard brick inside, and my stomach and head were also aching — I was trying very hard not to melt down. It was hard for me to even speak, and I didn't want to be with anyone. I just needed to be at home, I wanted to be with my girls, yet I needed to be alone. Someone may have rung my sister as she arrived to take me home.

I said my goodbyes and James' brothers walked us out to the car, one of them telling my sister he is feeling very sad for me. I didn't want to hear about it. Now I knew that my time with James and any future conversations with him were gone! Despite all my build-up and plans, I was a total wreck.

Later, I was further hurt when a friend of the family told me that she had drawn Mary's name for 'Secret Santa'. Mary was even on the family gift list! I had been asked a month before if I was still going on the list and was glad that I'd said that it was probably best not to. However, I still bought gifts for the little ones in the family.

I didn't expect James to stay alone for the rest of his life, but I was shocked how quickly he got involved with another woman. I was totally torn on the inside. This woman is not just a woman he sees at the local club and gives compliments to, he had already travelled that road. She sleeps in his arms

Chapter 19

every night, wakes with him every morning, and had been for seven months. I wondered how long he'd been seeing her before they moved in together, knowing that there had to be history.

I had given James far more credit than he deserved. So had Georgia and my sister. How could he do this to me? He knows how damaged I have been since my brain bleed! I never felt loved by him and now I know it to be true.

Christmas Day is always a bittersweet time when I put a lot behind me. I tend to get through the day by putting bad memories out of my head and enjoying the day with family, friends and lots of Christmas cheer. The end of that Christmas Day was like the ending of a horror day for me. Later when home, I walked to the cemetery to sit at the grave of James' father to tell him about my day. I told of my shock news, and I asked, 'What do you think of that?' As if on cue, at 6 pm my phone beeps with a message from James wishing me a merry Christmas and hoping I had a good day. I felt like an afterthought as Christmas Day was almost over. My tears didn't look out of place, and a man who works at the cemetery stopped his car beside me to tell me the gates would be locked in twenty minutes, so I had to leave.

On my walk home I was hoping to not see anyone because I am too unhappy to speak. I then reminded myself that the following day is my sister's birthday and I had organised lunch in a restaurant with some girlfriends. I wondered how

I would get through the day but realised it was better than staying home alone where I could become embroiled in my own thoughts. I knew I had to be there, so I decided to try and look forward to it.

Usually sleeping up to fourteen hours each night, this Christmas night I barely slept an hour. My mind was visualising James and Mary in bed together, my stupid images are probably normal, but they were painful, and I wondered again –why couldn't he tell me? I was hurting so deeply, feeling sick and alone.

I told myself that I must stop wondering what I did wrong and stop blaming myself. However, the day brought flashes of our times together over the years, and I assumed I was looking for a breakdown point to blame myself for. I wished we'd had a big fight, and I did something wrong so I could blame myself for him leaving me. I wished he'd told me, and I didn't have to find out about Mary like I had.

I wish, I wish, I wish.

Chapter 20

Boxing Day, and my sister's birthday has arrived. I have arranged a lunch with some friends, and I'll need to brace myself and be strong in order to not be a bother to anyone. I hadn't cried over James for a couple of years until yesterday, and now I am making up for lost time.

I am finding it hard to hide my hurt but won't allow myself to feel rejected or unworthy like I had in the past. I decided when I felt unloved, I'd think of the many days spent crying. Knowing I was with my sister and our shared friends — people who care — gave me a bit of strength to not allow my hurt to upset the day. Having already ruined Christmas, this day was not a good day for me to be crying.

During lunch, I was very sick and felt an aching in my chest, making it hard to eat. I tried to fit in with conversations and laughter but one of my friends noticed I was very quiet. 'What on earth has happened?' she asked, concerned, later explaining that I'd been the happiest she'd ever seen until then.

I told her of my news and began trembling. She had known for some time I'd suspected another woman but joined the other people who had told me I was wrong to think about James that way. On finding out that James had been living with another woman for seven months, my friend was shocked, suggesting that a separation would be good for me, and that in time, I would be happier.

Overhearing, another friend said it was a good thing he had a new woman because now I had no choice but to put him behind me, reminding me that she'd seen me upset on many occasions. Although good advice, I knew it was easier said than done. I began wondering, was Mary more loving than me? Was she a nicer person; happier and therefore, smiling more than me? On a downer, I agreed that yes, she was probably all of those things and more. Would she then become unhappy like I had been? She would never have the history I had, I decided, but a bitter thought came to mind: Is she *better* for him than me? I knew then she would grow unhappy and leave him.

My friend reminds me again how sad I had been with James, but I don't really need to be reminded how unhappy I was for so long. Without a second thought I have been replaced ... thanks James! While my friend is talking, my mind drifts over the years with James, my unhappiness on the inside running deep. Many nights I'd cry in bed and James would say I had a problem in my head, not realising that I actually did. He was partly right, but it was an emotional problem — I had felt unloved, and everything sprang from there.

Now, to somehow get past all this aching, I *had* to! I would not allow it to consume me any longer, especially since I'd worked so hard over a few years to recover from my medical scare. I had gained physical and (some) emotional strength and wasn't prepared to let James dissolve it all. I reminded myself that my life had become happy in the past couple of months with a realisation that, putting things in perspective, the loneliest I'd ever felt was the times I was with James!

As my friend's face moved into view again, I made an effort to enjoy the rest of our day at lunch with a knowing that my life would improve again — but that positive feeling was short-lived. Unable to sleep that night, I walked the streets until four in the morning, returning home with the inside of my mouth, lips and tongue bitten and bleeding. I had been unaware of doing this to myself while walking and thinking about James and his lack of respect.

Approaching seven years since my bleed, I concluded that if life changes every seven years like I'd heard, then I was due for a change and maybe this hurting would stop. I felt such a huge hurt-filled gap inside, one I knew that only I could change. I am solely accountable for my own smiles, no one else is going to put a smile on my face but me! All the thoughts and feelings of wanting to scream at James needed to be tossed out because he wasn't worth the energy expended in yelling at him.

With no guide but my own experience, I told myself that I must teach myself to repair emotionally, and not allow this setback to define me. My new life is a gift which I must embrace so I needed to throw out hurt and be glad to be alive. I reminded myself how lucky I have been to survive a brain haemorrhage and strokes.

Over the next few weeks, I developed mouth ulcers, and all I could do was to keep breathing, while my heart felt like it had been ripped out of my chest, leaving behind a huge black emptiness. Just for good measure, shingles returned. My inability to smile or eat, and volatile gastric attacks had brought about a huge drop in weight, but it was the return of headaches that terrified me. I began doing some serious walking, giving myself a good talking to along the way. The walks once again become my personal therapy to ease the inner torment. It wasn't long before I realised that despite the benefits of walking, I was once again absorbed in my own head space, unable to look at anyone directly — not good!

James was still constantly on my mind and knew I couldn't allow it to linger. I made a promise to remain mindful of my feelings and to make an effort to smile and say hi to people. I recognised that each day would present feelings that I didn't want to deal with, but as a responsible and well-balanced woman, it was up to me to work through them.

Ten months later, I was able to look at couples without imagining James and Mary together and desperately painting a picture of her in my mind. I began to think I am going to win this battle, as I didn't care about her looks, and pretty much, *she can keep him*! Over the years, people have told me

Chapter 20

that I must have survived a brain haemorrhage for a reason, but I wonder — was it to feel this heartache? Was it a learning experience?

Soon, each day bled into the next until a few months later Leigh in Toowoomba phoned me to tell me about my youngest grandson — the star football player. He had an accident and has broken his neck! Oh SHIT! I tried to comfort her and immediately told her I was coming up to be with her. I then told her that if a broken neck was meant to be in his life, it was better to happen now while he was young and had a better chance to achieve full repair from it. As usual, I didn't know what I was talking about, but I felt the need to appear to be the mum who is able to comfort and I didn't want to only say: 'There, there, he will be okay.' Perhaps learning this philosophy from my bleed, I further stated, 'Life has a way of making things happen to us just as they are meant to, and, at the time they are meant to.' Not fully understanding the situation, I assured Leigh that his break wouldn't cripple him, and hoped I was right. I encouraged her to try not to cry in front of him because, 'He needs to pull on your strength and at his age may feel like crying himself if he sees you crying.' I didn't quite know what else to say to make her feel better, but I told her to remain strong and positive and I was coming up there. Only two months previously, their entire town was ravaged by floods. Leigh and her children lost a friend who had been swept away in the raging waters and some friends had lost livestock, so it had been a horrible time for all concerned.

This had really put things in perspective for me with all my crying over James and Mary. How stupid of me to ache so much over a man, I should be rejoicing — isn't family so much more important?

A few days later I arrived in Toowoomba, pleased to find my grandson had been discharged from hospital and was expected to make a full recovery. He needed to wear a neck brace, not overheat his body, and avoid being knocked over, which meant no school and no exercise. I thought he wouldn't mind missing school, but the exercise which had become part of his everyday existence would be sorely missed. While staying with them, I was pleased to see he had a constant flow of friends visiting him, day and night. A good boy, he seemed to me to be very soft with an ability to express feelings of care and concern, which I found pleasing. His many wins in sport had not given him a big head. The knowledge of what could have happened had snapped me into reality, making me see that to cry over a man who had not shown me love was stupid, unnecessary and a waste of emotions. By crying, I was giving into it, which was a kind of acceptance, rather than escape.

After a time in Toowoomba catching up with my other grandchildren, and when all seemed to have settled down, it was time for me to return home to begin my new life, putting James out of my heart and my head. I left Toowoomba on the following Sunday and travelled by bus to the Gold Coast where I stayed with a friend who had moved there just after my bleed. It was nice to stay with her for five days. When I felt the need to return home, she convinced me to fly, and not be afraid. I flew home, not completely released of heartache about James, but now with a different perspective on things, knowing that there are far more important things to spend emotional energy on. There are things with love attached, and although I may take a while to recover from James, I will become a much stronger person. But I knew I must be careful, and along the way not become hard and bitter, just stronger of heart and wiser. I have come through so much more and hasn't that made me stronger?

A few months later, I began to brace myself when I found out that James and I were invited to the same friend's event. James had accepted, which would be a huge test for me. I wondered if he would try to come near me to talk to me, maybe to say sorry? Oh God, who was I kidding! Will he bring Mary?

Before the day of the party, I had to rid myself of any material reminders I had of him. I had thrown out other things from him and had kept a few things that were more special. Aside from the dress I'd bought for our wedding was a little wind-up carousel figurine, a gift to me on our first date over twenty-four years ago. I was unable to bring myself to throw it away, so I may give it to someone special, most probably his mother, while the dress will be sold. I hoped that I would heal in the very near future.

My days are mostly spent with friends like Georgia, Ruby, Anne and my sister. My life seems to have opened up in so many areas and I have discovered an awareness of how I am affected by events in my life, sometimes taking things into a place very deep inside. I learn that I must develop an ability to manage my emotions and I admit to myself that I am looking forward to seeing James. I have strange expectations of how it will pan out.

One week to go! I must stop these stupid self-sabotaging thoughts; I see the need to pull myself together. I have developed so much mental strength since my bleed, and apart from some anxious feelings when first home from hospital, I have avoided any depression that many expected to overcome me. I think again about my friend's advice at the lunch that maybe James and I needed to split. We hadn't been a couple for many years, and I'd been sad for so long before that, so maybe my tears are due to me hating to fail.

I have now made a decision — do I want my children to see me crying? Do I want *anyone* to see me crying for that matter? I tell myself that living with another woman is a good thing for James and I will soon be happy. I had always felt overlooked by James but in an effort to move forward, I wondered how I was going to drag myself through each day. I knew I had to get myself get out the door, on a train, a bus — anything. My walking took on a whole new meaning as I thought a lot about my life and of the ordeal from the past years.

Chapter 20

Over the following weeks, my weight dropped to a mere forty-nine kilograms, and I had no façade to shield me. I am unable to pretend, so everyone can see my unhappiness. I don't care though as I need to be true to myself. Even months later, still recovering, I cry when in bed thinking of James. I wonder again, as I had in the past, did he ever really care? Did I become too much work for him; too needy?

We had travelled through so much in our years together and although Mary won't have the history with him that I had, I hope he gives her more appreciation than he gave me.

Months later, Sundays in church meant seeing all the happy couples together, which would prompt me to leave early as it showed in sharp relief my need to be on my own. I also didn't want to be a bother to my girls, so when my best friend Georgia returned from a holiday overseas, I went to see her. When I was telling her about James, I began to shake uncontrollably, and I needed to be sick, which left me hating myself for becoming so upset. I'd tried to avoid a meltdown, so I told myself that I needed all my emotions to be able to mend. I began to get cramps in my head, scared what may be going on in there so I rang my doctor, who told me it would be best to ring Dr Chandler. I didn't want to annoy him, so I chose to ride it out and after a few days they stopped.

Although I don't want to be a cold person, I need to unload a lot of my emotions as I begin to think that they are my enemy. I wish I could hit or smash something. I feel rage, anger and hurt inside, so I begin to wonder about becoming a shallow person because shallow people don't seem to get hurt, because shallow people don't really care about others. If I am shallow too, I will be in a different head space with no heart feelings, just head thoughts. Something has to work. Maybe, if I never mention James' name again, I will trick my brain and it will think he no longer exists in my world, so I will rid myself of him ...

Before I close him out of my life, I will write to him and tell him how I had suspected another woman and ask why he couldn't have been honest with me. I don't want to think about the whys though. After two weeks of careful wording, I sent a letter, which came back in a week RTS with his local post office stamp on it. I then sent a text message asking why he had sent it back to me, and he came undone with his bullshit reply of having never received it. I promised myself I would not slip into a bad space.

Over the following few weeks, I waited for the heartache to ease and stayed aware to not slip into any depression because I had been in a dark place for many years and knew only too well how hard it is to get out from such a place.

The day before the party that we'd both been invited to, I saw James' brother, who was also invited, and who told me James intended to speak to me when he saw me at the party. Inwardly, I bristled at James' audacity — so now I am meant to speak to him because it suits him? *I don't think so, James.*

I told his brother to tell him to stay as far away from me as

Chapter 20

possible. 'I am not interested in what he has to say any more. Maybe in his next life, he will learn to appreciate and respect the people who love him, and the party is just too convenient for him!'

When the day of the party arrived, I surprised myself by steeling up and smiled with other friends in conversations. James kept a distance from me staying on the other side of the room, choosing not to acknowledge me, not even a hello. What did I expect? I knew I must get over this aching inside.

Walking brought about more thoughts about James and the more upset I became, the faster I walked. When I realised how walking is not good for someone who is losing too much weight, I put my walking on hold, hoping to gain some.

Nobody was aware of the torment going on inside my head and once again I was unable to smile and say hello to people passing me in the street because I couldn't look anyone in the eye. Why again? I won't let this happen again! I don't want to carry emotional pain and I realise that life is a combination of good and bad, so I need to be able to carry those feelings and not allow the bad to consume and weigh me down. My crying has to stop. I felt as though every organ inside me from waist up to neck was damaged and sore because I had allowed my hurt to consume me. In order to get myself past all of the aching inside that I was feeling, I had to change my obsessive nature because I began to sink and lose the desire to go anywhere, just in case I saw someone I knew.

My head was full of thoughts and reeling with curious questions. Why this? Why that? I felt so damaged. Is this depression? If so, it can get out of my life — I don't need it! I was emotionally charged up so why not put it to good use and empower myself?

Over the following few weeks, I began taking lots of train rides as I'd done in my youth, so I was at least entertained by the goings-on around me, and I didn't present as a chore for my friends or any of my daughters to repair. One day while on the train, I sat next to a woman James and I both knew. She asked me how it had gone seeing James at the recent party. When my stomach began to turn, I had to tell her that the less I spoke of James the better, saying, 'I need to get past him!', not sharing with her that I struggled so with that very thing. Building to a crescendo, I began to throw up on the train. I was embarrassed because the train was full of school kids and workers, and they all moved away. My friend saw how affected I was by things that had happened, particularly as I'd cleared the carriage. When the next station came, I quickly got off, desperate to escape the unpleasant situation. Surprisingly, my friend got off the train with me, saying how sorry she was and that she hadn't realised I was so upset.

Later that night while going over the incident as part of my personal therapy session, I told myself how I needed to pull myself together. *I can't let myself get to throw-up stage ever again*! I tried telling myself it was only my pride that was hurting, which led me to question if I was allowing my pride destroy me. Was I so full of pride I couldn't step over it? When will it end? Although raw and hurting, I knew that everything has an ending so one day my hurting would also have an ending and, in the meantime, I have learnt much from my time spent with, and without, James.

Thanks to modern technology, when I do need to speak with James, I am able to avoid speaking in person, and can contact him via cyber space, most of which he only answers on occasion. In an attempt to divert my ache, Joanne bought me a book to read which was written by a head and neck surgeon, Dr Chris O'Brien, who sadly had been diagnosed with a brain tumour and was dying. He developed a proposal to transform the Sydney Cancer Centre into a world-class comprehensive cancer centre — Lifehouse. I was enjoying reading about him and gained a lot of positive information and help from his writing. I began to feel like I knew him, so he was no longer just the surgeon who wrote the book, but now a friend. I became more and more upset by his writings though and was unable to finish reading his book. Joanne tells me that out of respect for him, I should try to finish it; one day when I am feeling stronger and better able to accept his situation, I will.

I have travelled through many emotions over the past few years and found that my best parts have emerged from my darkest and most painful areas. I need to learn how to get out of my own way and am often thinking of my head and heart travels over the recent nine years. My father, if watching down on me, will most probably wish he had never told me to not trust God or an Asian man; the same two things that saved me and helped me to recover. I understand my father's attitude and am still going to church each week to thank God for the things dad had told me to dislike and not trust.

As though I needed reminding of my own luck, I received a phone call with news of my neighbour Monique, who was the friend I had thought Dr Chandler was speaking to me about nine years previously, when in actual fact it was *me* he was speaking about.

Monique had spent twenty-five years in a body that stopped working for her after a cerebral bleed followed by a series of strokes; the same as had happened to me. The phone call informs me that she has died. It is very sad for her family, yet I am certain that they will find her release a blessing, for in death she is freed. Free from her entrapment that was her life on earth, she is now able to spread her wings and fly.

Chapter 21

All things have an ending as I had come to appreciate. I am now pleased to know that all the writing I have done for now, has ended. Along with it, so have the nightmares that arose from disturbed memory files, opened in the course of writing these pages. I have learned very much about myself during what became almost ten years for me to complete.

Glad to have found the woman inside who was lost for so many years, this is the time that I met myself. The woman I am today is a far different woman to the one who wrote the first few pages. I have the hard-won realisation after all these years that I am *not* ugly, or bitter, and am far from negative. I also know that I never had a problem in my head other than a medical one. The problem actually lay in my heart and was of the emotional kind. This is not to say I consider myself wrong or sensitive, I simply think more people should have sensitivity of the emotional kind.

I no longer live with rejected energy, and I am no longer judgmental of myself due to self-doubt, and now, away from

James, I am emotionally stronger and more aware of my strengths; strong enough to avoid weaknesses that may come into play. I have learned that the 'emotional' things in life that frightened me became the things that pushed me along to complete these pages, so I now welcome those feelings that have been my teachings. I am tearing down the walls I had built around myself for protection from pain and I no longer self-examine with a lens of bad feelings that *I* had allowed to hold me hostage. I have now recognised my own value and have found hidden and suppressed strengths, able to reinforce them with a knowing I will no longer be moulded by my emotions or by other people. I am no longer living in the bubble I had been in for so many years before my brain bleed, now happy to say I no longer find happy people annoying!

I have not only learnt about myself but have also learnt about other people. Some people I had placed on a pedestal, conveniently fulfilling for them their desire to be there. I don't auto-place people up there now, that is something that needs to be earned. I now see a person in her or his true light and from my perspective; not what others wish me to see. I had been easily conned and silly to allow this; however, had it not been for the cons and upsets, perhaps my eyes would be still veiled.

Time has, at last, returned to a normal span for me so I no longer have the occasional Ground Hog Day. I used to feel like a day had frozen and lasted a month but with no memory of the day's events. Some days seemed to end as soon as they

Chapter 21

began; I felt there had been no hours or minutes in each day. Time was on a different span while I was in a parallel life. Now I no longer need to go into a newsagency and view the front page to find out which day I am in. I no longer have bad days, I only have a bad 'time' that may last for an hour or so, sometimes less.

I still want to achieve so much more in this body that has trouble doing things as it was able to before all this. I am lucky I can live alone and look after myself — I can do up my shoelaces, put my bra on, get back into my jeans and do up a zipper, *and* wear trackpants with a tie in front. Some days I am emotional and feel like I carry wounds that are not visible on the outside yet are still very profound on the inside; I am happy to have them and have learnt from them and now stopped beating myself up over my emotions.

I welcome them now and am able to place them in the right space, so they don't destroy my days. I now know that life is not about getting everything 'right', and in fact, getting it wrong sometimes and having to work through some things can only make us a better person.

My recovery, both physically and emotionally, has been a long, slow and painful experience for me. I am now pleased to have completed eighty per cent of the repair process. I enjoy living alone, and spending quality time with my girls, the kind of daughters that most mothers dream to have, who make me proud, all with good careers. Each one of them is a good wholesome woman and a good mum to their children.

During the course of writing these pages, I have become a grandmother for the eighth, ninth and tenth time, and am now expecting my eleventh! My relationship with each of my girls is unique and we spend precious hours together. I am still attending the gym twice a week, doing yoga as well as all the other gym stuff and I walk every day, still loving to feel the warm sun on my body. My life with all of its ups and downs and in-betweens has made me into the person I have become. I have put away most of my hurt, so am no longer living with unhappiness and tears every day. My 'worst parts' have also been put away somewhere and I don't need to know where because I don't want them! All of my experiences and events, some good, some not so good, have each been a step in a learning, helping *me* to grow into *me*.

I am still learning about my many emotions, some of which I wish I didn't have, but like them or not, they are mine and I need them in order to carry a certain depth of empathy, love and concern. Even my anger, coupled with adrenalin, has been necessary for my emotive repairs.

Finally, after almost six long years of aching over James, I tell myself that I have repaired emotionally, because he is no longer an issue for me. He and Mary have long been separated, although I view this from a different place now. No longer do I cry over him. No longer am I pushing sad feelings away in order to prevent my happy space becoming invaded. I will never again wear rose-coloured glasses and am becoming good at turning a negative into a positive! I like to think that my brain haemorrhage was a good thing, and indeed, a much-needed turning point to bring about the many changes in my life, making it better than it has been in many years. Does that mean I was right when I told my daughter (after her son broke his neck) that all things happen in our lives just at the time when they are meant to, and hopefully when we'll benefit most?

In fact, as stated above, the very thing that almost killed me is the thing that saved me. I still struggle physically when I am tired, which causes me to limp and also to slur my words because my tongue feels like it weighs a ton. Now, I know that life is not about getting it all right because not many of us do! Life is just about staying happy ... because we can be!

Chapter 22

Friday will be my final visit with Dr Chandler as I have been told that he is soon to retire. I wonder if and when I will ever see him again. I am sure his retirement will upset a lot of people but of course I think I am more upset than anyone else, and with my stupid deep emotions, I most likely am just that! My girlfriends have joked with me and told me I have had a crush on Dr Chandler, and if I am going to be true with myself, I could say that if my overwhelming respect and appreciation is a crush, then yes, I have had a crush on him, which would explain why I had been in awe of him. I'm sure this is a normal feeling with highly emotive people such as me! Underneath my selfishness, I am happy for him to be retiring.

When the day came for my final consultation with Dr Chandler, I was feeling very sad, concerned that I may cry, which would be silly of me and most likely would embarrass this humble man who has been gifted into my life. On my final visit to him, I forgot to tell him about all the things that I had achieved in the past year since my last consultation.

Chapter 22

Instead, I mentioned on how some days I was feeling a bit sad. Why did I do that? Especially when it's the opposite and I am happy most days.

So now, he most likely thinks I am not as well as I really am. I think I stuffed up because I was so nervous. Being pissed off with myself is nothing unusual for me, as I've felt that way many times over the past seven years.

Later, while traveling home on the train, I tried to hold back my tears, but I was so sad on that day and far too emotive. Traveling home during busy peak hour, I was crying. I imagine people must have assumed something horrible had happened to that poor woman. Well, it had! I was sad because I didn't think I would ever see Dr Chandler again. I have now learnt how a person can love someone of the opposite sex without being in love with them. This feeling I have is not a passionate love; it's more a respect with overwhelming admiration. I needed to accept his retirement respectfully and with maturity. I have been blessed to have had such a clever and wonderful man come into my life, so unexpectedly, and I am grateful for whatever and whoever made it happen. He became the reason I wanted to reach many goals and I always had great excitement thinking about telling him of my achievements, which sometimes I would forget to do, being so in awe of him. I had been unable to take my eyes off his clever hands, thinking they had been working on my brain and repaired so much. While deep in thought, I would forget almost all of the things I wanted to tell him and I let my nerves get the better of me, but I am grateful to have been able to have had the past ten years in which I looked forward to my yearly consultations with him. Always grateful he was sent into my life, now, I must let go of him and begin to achieve things for myself. I will miss him, and while I'm not about to beat myself up over this, I realise that perhaps I am too sensitive.

Today, on the day of my last visit to him, the child in me is feeling very sad, so my intelligence tells me I haven't changed very much; still very much needing to coach myself in my emotive spaces, still obsessing and taking things down to a deep level that is not good for me. I understand that it's just me, it's who I am, the way I am. I didn't know me for so long when so much of me had been pressed away for so many years leading up to my bleed.

Epilogue

Over the years that I spent writing these pages, I have seen many changes. The house I grew up in from age three has now been demolished, replaced with medium density dwellings. Also, the house that belonged to friends of my parents, where I was able to live for protection for six weeks, the same house I would pass and reflect about the agave plants on my way to the train station, is also gone, now replaced with high-rise dwellings. In happier days, the building that James and I, along with his family, renovated and had a thriving business in, is now also gone, currently having high-rises built on the grounds. The Princes Highway that we crossed every day on horseback is now four lanes each way and would be impossible to cross now, certainly not by anyone on horseback. The biggest change that I recognise is a change within — I have changed and learned to like me. I now have a grand memory and I am so happy and grateful to be alive and well. I'm grateful to still be here with happy daughters and grandchildren; happy to be my own friend because some days when I need a friend, it's only me around!

While writing these pages I have met myself, raw and exposed; my life is all written and all that's left now is embracing who I am! My mind is no longer behaving like a sieve, and I realise that life throws good and bad at us which can teach us who we are. I have learned to remain aware of how I am feeling, and I try to not drop the ball emotionally. I feel I have grown and no longer trapped in an emotional vacuum. The only person whom I should seek approval from is me, myself. Importantly, although I must be careful to not become hard or uncaring, I will not allow emotional love to be so important to me. I will make better choices in the future, and for now, will avoid any intimacy. I am enjoying my life with a love of every day. Able to do, and enjoy, so much, I'm just living for myself with the best part knowing that my girls are all well and happy with healthy and well-behaved children of their own. I sleep at least ten hours every night, sometimes even more. I no longer wonder what my life has in store for me, accepting that it is what it is.

I have not had a cramp in my head for some time now, so I enjoy each day, grateful that I am able to put my feet on the ground and stand up; I consider that even a bad day is a good day for me. *What a blessing.* It was not my intent to gain from my writing because it was not about closure. I don't believe in that word anyway because it is a word that I find doesn't have any real meaning. Do we *ever* get closure? That would equate to being a loss of memory, wouldn't it? Nor was my writing for healing or as a release, but my journey began when writing was all that I could do alone in my damaged body.

I won't allow my hurts to define me, and these days, because I am unable to drive, I still travel by bus or train. When crossing the road, I am now able to stay within the lines of the pedestrian crossings (all two metres width of them), finding it amusing to remember how I was unable to stay within the markings when I escaped from home for a trip out alone. It was little wonder I looked drunk stepping outside the pedestrian stripes. Also, another venture I find pleasing is getting up the many steps at the railway station. *Simple*! I can overtake and can take two steps at a time if I want. I am so pleased at how far my healing has progressed — from my first attempt at home when getting up sixteen steps into my bedroom took me almost an hour on my hands and knees and exhausted me to tears, followed with a sixteen-hour sleep. I am no longer falling into a progression of physical or verbal mistakes, and if I could, I would change only one thing in my life, which would, no doubt, bring about other changes!

I have learnt to 'unhurt' myself by getting out of my own way, and I no longer waste my days thinking about James and the years we were together. I still hurt deeply with the way things ended, but after all the passing years, I realise that most likely I'll always hurt over that and will never understand. So, to be true to myself I must be aware that I most likely won't ever get over James, even though at times when I was with him, I was not a happy person, but I have learnt that this ache comes with my depth of character. I'm also glad now that I didn't become that shallow person when I thought it may prevent me from any more hurt. I won't immerse myself in another person's world.

No longer do I wonder why things happen, as some things seem to have no reason. Yet I still believe that all events happen because they are *meant* to happen, that *nothing* is a random event because *everything* is a part of our journey. Ultimately, we may never know the reason behind the things that happen, we just need to be able to accept that they do. Over the years I have wondered why my son died. I think of him very often and have never found a proper reason for his taking, but told myself that if my son had lived, I may not have had my last child. Is she here for a reason? Was my son's death not about him leaving, but instead, about making way for my next child? I still feel the loss of him, and the birth of my own grandchildren has each been a tender time for me, the birth of each boy bringing curious thoughts — would my own son have looked like one of the boys? Which one?

These days, in order to accept things as they are, I will pull good out of a bad situation. Darkness can be a good teacher. I have also learnt a lot about my emotions and hope, if needed, that I will be able to comfort others. My brain haemorrhage only killed the woman I had become while I was living in the world of others — not me! I am now the woman I was *born* to be.

Although still not so good, my (fine) motor skills are very much improved, with other skills returning, and I am pleased that my left hand is no longer locked in a claw-like form on the end of my arm, twisted across my stooped body. I am pleased that my left side is now responding to requests from my brain and no longer has a mind of its own. Before this, we all referred to it as 'thing' because it was like the hand on the television show The Adams Family who had a hand called 'thing' that had to be kept on a cabinet because it didn't respond to orders and couldn't be trusted. it did silly things all on its own just like mine would do at times when my hand was just like that I am now aware of my hands attached to the lower part of my arms, and without looking, I know how far I can reach to grab something and can place something evenly, so it won't fall again. I am no longer fearful of my pants falling down since I can now wear fitted slacks, able to do up a zipper or buttons and able to tie a cord at the waist if need be. However, I still am unable to successfully wear some types of shoes — thongs and slip-ons fly off my feet like weapons because I have no automatic pilot working for my toes to grip and keep these kinds of shoes on. My left side still tires so much, so I limp when my body is tired, yet I can walk for miles and miles. I no longer spend a lot of my days getting caught up in a progression of mistakes, both verbal and physical, or emotional, but still sound a little drunk when I'm tired and my tongue becomes very heavy.

I am still attending church every week, knowing so much

more now. I recall watching a movie called *The Color Purple*, where one of the ladies in it said to another lady, 'I think it pisses God off if you walk by the color purple in a field somewhere and don't notice it.' Well, I don't think that I have pissed God off yet, because I never walk past anything purple without noticing it and thinking of my mother.

I consider myself one of the lucky people of this world for more reasons than I can list. And I don't give in to occasional feelings of being a lost soul. I look forward to what my life has in store for me next. When I go to bed each night, I look forward to the next day. If a challenge arises — bring it on, I will deal with it. Looking back, I have a realisation that when I began writing I was a tortured soul who, so far, had made no sense of her own life. The woman writing this final page, is not the same woman who wrote those first telling words. This one is a happier, wiser and more confident woman.

Sadly though, my capacity to forgive has somewhat lessened; but I have found satisfaction within myself and will no longer allow the behaviour of others to break my spirit. I know me now and will no longer live in another's world. I will live in MY world, in MY headspace. The only thing that saddens me is that I don't think I am capable of love ... so that's disappointing, but necessary!

www.ingramcontent.com/pod-product-compliance
Lightning Source LLC
Chambersburg PA
CBHW020136130526
44590CB00039B/190